THE MEMOIRS OF PRINCESS ALICE, DUCHESS OF GLOUCESTER

Eightieth birthday portrait, 1982,
by my sister-in-law, Lady George Scott.

THE MEMOIRS OF PRINCESS ALICE, DUCHESS OF GLOUCESTER

COLLINS
8 Grafton Street, London W1
1983

William Collins Sons and Co. Ltd.
London · Glasgow · Sydney · Auckland
Toronto · Johannesburg

BRITISH LIBRARY CATALOGUING IN PUBLICATION DATA

Alice, *Princess, Duchess of Gloucester*
The memoirs of Princess Alice, Duchess of Gloucester
1. Alice, *Princess, Duchess of Gloucester*
2. Great Britain – Princes and Princesses – Biography
I. Title
941.082'092'4   DA566.9./
ISBN 0-00-216646-1

First published 1983
© H.R.H. Princess Alice, Duchess of Gloucester 1983
Reprinted June 1983

Photoset in Bembo by
Rowland Phototypesetting Ltd
Bury St Edmunds, Suffolk
Printed in Great Britain by
St Edmundsbury Press, Bury St Edmunds, Suffolk

Illustrations

Prelude

When I was about fourteen, my mother took the younger children to a place called Seascale on the Cumberland shore of the Solway Firth. Mary and I lost no time in putting on our bathing things and rushing down to the beach. The tide was right out. The two of us walked and walked in about a foot of water. At last it got a little deeper so I said: 'I'll go on till I'm up to my waist and then you swim out to me.' I could not swim very well, and Mary was just learning. So on I went – and suddenly a wave came. I found myself up to my neck, then out of my depth. I shouted to Mary to go back, but she had not come as far as I had and had already turned and was splashing for shore.

I swam and swam, but it was no good. Whenever I searched with my toes for the bottom there was a frightening void. I guessed I was in the grip of a current. Apparently there had been a sign saying 'Beware of Currents', but I had not noticed it. My mother had no other grown-up with her, and as she came on to the beach, she noticed the sign and to her horror saw us far out. Some women passed by and, distraught, she asked them to help. They said they could not see what they could do. In the meantime I began to feel too tired to go on: 'I'll drown and be done with it,' I thought.

So I gave up – and the shock of half-drowning must have brought me to my senses. 'I don't want to die! I'm so young. Surely I'm too young to die now! I have hardly had any life.' And I prayed: 'Oh God, give me my life. I promise I'll make use of it if you give it back to me.' The next instant my feet touched rocks. I was able to stand up and get my breath back. I had been carried quite a way down the coast – some houses had come and gone on my left – but the rocks proved to be a reef and I was able to scramble through them back to shallow water without further mishap.

My mother was furious – 'How could you do such a foolish thing! You might have drowned your sister as well as yourself! I've never had such a fright!' and so on – which was not very comforting. But the incident changed my life. For years it haunted me. I had made a covenant. In return for my life I had promised to dedicate it to some useful purpose; but there never seemed to be anything that required my help or that I was any use at. So when, through a series of unforeseen circumstances, I one day found myself allotted a life of public duty in the service of my country, a very secret pledge was honoured.

1

CAN IT REALLY BE eighty years since I made my first appearance into this world, on Christmas Day, 1901, at Montagu House, Whitehall, London? Apart from my three sisters and an aged cousin of ninety-five I doubt if there is anyone now alive who can remember the place. It stood more or less opposite the gateway into Horse Guards Parade, and was demolished in favour of government offices well over half a century ago. Recently, as Air Chief Commandant of the W.A.A.F., I had cause to be in these new premises and somewhat startled a gathering of Air Women when I announced that I had been born just below where we were all sitting! This was absolutely true, for I can well remember my mother's corner bedroom overlooking the river and being told that it was there that I was born. She must have found the timing of my arrival singularly inconvenient, not least because the family traditionally assembled at Dalkeith for Christmas. My childhood memories are dominated by houses, because every year, on a fixed rota, we used to visit different ones at different seasons. We lived in Montagu House from June till July.

The site was Crown property. One of the Dukes of Montagu first built a mansion there to save him the journey to his principal residence in Bloomsbury when he was kept late at the House of Lords. To travel a mile through London in those days was considered far too dangerous after dark. My great-grandfather commissioned the building that replaced it, which was completed in 1864. It was a large house with a big garden at the back extending to the Embankment, a gravel sweep at the front with a porter's lodge at the main gates, and a row of high trees hiding the traffic as it passed along Whitehall. There were no attics or basement. The top two floors were devoted to bedrooms, the first floor to sitting rooms and reception rooms and the ground floor to the kitchens and servants' quarters. The main reception rooms all gave on to a wide stone terrace, with steps at either end descending to the garden. Beyond the garden you could see the Thames.

My memories are of a very large house, which of course it was. There must have been a great number of bedrooms, for during the summer season not only my parents and, eventually, the eight of us children stayed there, but also my aunt Katie Hampden (my father's eldest sister) and her husband and children. There were also, of course, my grandparents and my aunt Connie, their second youngest child, who, before her marriage to Douglas Cairns, acted as a general factotum to her parents. The grown-ups each had a maid or valet. Two nurses, a nursery maid and a governess supervised me and my brothers and sisters. All told there were sixty-eight people permanently resident during the season – and, as far as I know, only one bathroom in the whole building. I cannot remember who was allowed to use it! Our nurseries and schoolroom were on the second-floor, alongside the other main bedrooms and dressing-rooms; the Brand cousins had their nurseries on the top floor with a wonderful view over the Embankment and the river. One could hear the trams rattling past and the booming and hoots of the ships travelling up and down the Thames.

My grandparents presided, and I can remember them during the Montagu House summers in some ways better than I can my parents. This is not altogether surprising. My father was an MP and rarely got home before our bedtime, and my mother hated the season. She was a shy, retiring person, who never came to the nurseries and always seemed to be busy in her own little sitting-room. Occasionally we would be allowed in but I disliked it because one always had to be quiet and do a jig-saw puzzle or something equally boring. On the whole, as young children, we seldom saw our parents.

My grandmother, in contrast, could not possibly have been more sociable. She entertained enormously, with masses of friends and relations pouring in and out for lunch-parties and dinner-parties. There was a custom, apparently established by my great-grandparents, that anyone who knew the family could turn up for lunch without invitation. My aunt Connie, in a private memoir she wrote, says that this custom was very popular with the denizens of Whitehall, from Prime Ministers downwards, and that up to twenty extra guests were daily catered for. I recall only two extra places being laid in this way. Perhaps entertainment was already becoming less lavish. It was a nice custom, especially for people who were not well off and had not got a cook themselves. The two empty chairs were invariably filled.

At one such pre-War lunch I remember that for the first time in my life I saw a woman – the morganatic wife of the Grand Duke Michael of Prussia – smoke a cigarette. She fitted the cigarette into the end of a long holder and then, to our amazement, had it lit. Nor was that all. My mother, who was presiding, had ordered mince, which she was keen on for some reason. When the dish was offered to the Grand Duke he said, very haughtily: 'No thank you. I prefer to chew my own meat.' There were always huge lunch-parties. The schoolroom table was set apart from the rest; there we sat with a governess and had to wait our turn till the grown-ups had been served, which took ages. If there were treats, like strawberries and cream, we would suffer agonies in case they were finished before reaching us. The butlers and footmen always tried to make sure there was something left over for us. We had great fun with them, though the only place in the servants' quarters which we were regularly allowed to visit was the still-room, to make cakes.

One memorable evening we were woken up at about ten o'clock to watch my grandparents going off to some court function in the Buccleuch state coach – my grandmother was Mistress of the Robes to Queen Alexandra. The coach was ornate and magnificent, and only used for important occasions like court balls or the Opening of Parliament. The harness was shining silver and there were a wigged coachman and footman in front and two postillions behind all in livery, with red breeches and white stockings. The family coat-of-arms, picked out in fairy-lights, had been mounted for the occasion over the front door – I distinctly remember this being lit electrically, though I do not think there was electric lighting in the house at that date. The coach subsequently went to a museum in Maidstone, but today it can be seen at Boughton in Northamptonshire, a Buccleuch residence in England. My nephew Johnnie, the present Duke, has been trying to find some stuffed horses for it so that the public can see the magnificent uniforms and harness as they were intended to be seen, but so far he has met with no success.

Each morning at Montagu House we used to visit our grandparents. My grandmother would be in her lovely sitting-room, with its blue satin chairs. She always looked very grand. My grandfather usually gave us half-a-crown or a sweet. We just went in and said 'Good Morning' before our morning walk; then we would scamper down the huge, slippery, white marble staircase into the hall. The hall was paved in white marble with inlaid black corners, and we used to enjoy jumping from one of these black 'islands' to the next. Footmen, wearing livery, sat on two mahogany benches, ready to open the door or answer bells. The prams were hidden somewhere to one side and the footmen used to help our nurses down the steps with them. A troop of little Scotts would then cross Whitehall and go into St James's Park to feed bread to the ducks, making faces on the way at the mounted sentries guarding the entrance to Horse Guards' Parade. I and my four sisters were invariably dressed alike in spite of the fourteen years difference between the eldest and youngest. On wet days we were put into little red mackintoshes which caused great amusement as we marched past the soldiers, because when it was raining they wore the same. Our prams, like the various household coaches, were decorated with the family crest and painted in the Buccleuch colours: dark green with a pale green line. The Fitzwilliam family, who lived next door in

Richmond Terrace (alas no more), had bright yellow prams and coaches, which we thought much smarter and envied greatly.

Mr Shotter was our lodge-keeper, an impeccably dressed old gentleman in a top hat. He would open the main gates in answer to a push-bell, but a side gate for people entering on foot could be opened automatically by treading on a little pedal outside. It was always a great game to tread on this pedal and hide out of sight before Mr Shotter could spot us – a phenomenon shortly explained, no doubt, by the arrival of a breathless nanny or governess in hot pursuit. Mr Shotter was a true friend, always playing with gusto his part as a man baffled by an inexplicable mystery.

Occasionally we would be taken for a drive with our mother to drop visiting cards. It was the custom to thank one's host and hostess the day after a party by dropping cards. Usually the coachman and footman would be despatched to do this, but occasionally, probably because she had nothing better to do, my mother, taking some of us, went along also. There was a very precise etiquette involved. One large card and two little ones had to be left, twisted over. The large one had 'The Countess of Dalkeith' engraved on it, the smaller ones 'The Earl of Dalkeith' – two 'Earls' had to go with one 'Countess' for some reason. No message was written on the cards. The footman would jump off and, on entering the particular house, would leave the cards on a tray provided in the hall. Meanwhile we would sit waiting in the carriage.

Other times, after tea, my mother would take us in the landau to Hyde Park – a landau was an open carriage with a hood that could go up if it rained. We would stop near Hyde Park Corner and go and sit on little green metal chairs that were set out under the trees. One hired the use of these uncomfortable seats by buying a ticket for tuppence from a ticket collector. Each day had a different colour, so that people could not cheat by using the same ticket twice. Various boring old gentlemen in top hats and tailcoats would then perch themselves alongside my mother and make polite conversation. We anticipated the whole procedure with a certain amount of dread. One evening as we plop-plopped along in the shadow of the fat coachman and the thin footman, this ritual was transformed by the sudden appearance of a fire-engine, with bells ringing, pulled by six black horses at full gallop. Our fat horses, enthused by the unexpected competition, tried their best to follow and were only checked with difficulty. It was a rather alarming moment.

Our greatest enjoyment was the garden. On one side of the lawn was a beautiful old Chinese pagoda, now at Boughton, in which my grandparents used to take tea, weather permitting; otherwise we seemed to have the whole place to ourselves. There were a few large plane trees, a catalpa tree, bushes and bordering flowerbeds. The flowers were for the most part red geraniums and marguerites encircled by close-planted clumps of those little royal-blue plants one always sees in public gardens. All other London gardens that we visited looked exactly the same. At the far end, there was a thick line of shrubs, a narrow path and then, bordering the Embankment, a seven foot wall with a wide top. We children (thought to be safely out of mischief in the garden) would pile chairs against it and clamber up to watch the passing traffic on the street and the ships beyond, so much more numerous in those days. We dangled wobbly wire spiders on long bits of elastic in the path of pedestrians below, skilfully whisking them up and ducking out of sight before our victims could spot us. There were always a number of pavement-artists sitting opposite, who could not have provided a more appreciative audience for our escapades. Afterwards we carefully put back the chairs exactly where we had found them. The garden had other attractions. Near the wall we each had a little allotment to tend. To get into the garden we had to go along a narrow passage past the housekeeper's room. This was always a treat, because she would let us choose something from her store of chocolates and sugar fruits as we passed.

On Sundays we were taken to church in the private chapel at Marlborough House. Queen Alexandra was usually there. She gave a children's party every year and at one of them a lot of pygmies danced about naked, which we thought very funny. For weeks my sister Sybil and I used to get into trouble for jumping

[14]

about without any clothes when we were meant to have been tucked up for the night. On the whole we did not do much visiting or party-going. Our numbers, Scotts and Brands combined, made us self-sufficient and never at a loss for amusement.

A memorable pastime was to send semaphore flag signals from the schoolroom balcony to the policemen across the way in Scotland Yard. They jovially signalled answers to our messages. Government offices were already predominant in the district, and Montagu House was taken over as an adjunct to the War Office during the war. My parents made do with a flat, and towards the end of the War bought 2 Grosvenor Place. By then the world too had changed out of all recognition.

2

Wʜᴇɴ ᴏᴜʀ ᴠɪsɪᴛ to London came to an end in July we abandoned Montagu House and set off by train for our own home at Eildon in the Borders. This journey was always a source of the keenest excitement, though rather long and tedious for a child. A happy moment came when the train used to stop somewhere south of Penrith to fill up with water, and our Nanny would open the window and let us hang our heads out to breathe in the first scent of the moors, while the engine up ahead hissed gently in the silence. Amongst clumps of heather, the bog cotton and little wild flowers – scabious and hare bells – bobbed and blew in the breezes and we knew that Scotland and our destination were not far off. All of us were rabid nationalists. We felt we belonged far more to Scotland than England. Everything Scottish was wonderful, everything English quite dreadful!

Eildon Hall, near St Boswells in Roxburghshire, was our first home; a Georgian house with Victorian additions, made from the local coral pink sandstone, and situated in a particularly attractive position at the foot of the Eildon Hills. From its windows there is a wonderful view of the valley below stretching away to the Cheviots thirty miles distant – that range of hills that for centuries has marked the border between Scotland and England. Across these fields and woods the colour would be forever changing under the sun and cloud shadows.

My earliest memory of all is of Eildon. I am in the nursery having a bath in a tin tub. Two brothers rush in fighting and one kicks off a boot, which lands with a splash in the water. The nursery maid is furious. I am frightened. This must have been when I was two. Eildon and its surrounding woods was very safe for children and we could roam wherever we liked.

My father was the local Member of Parliament and equally occupied by his directorships of the North British Railway and the Bank of Scotland, so we children seldom saw him except for lunch on Sunday. Our mother was at home but my memories of her are almost equally few. She seemed to be always resting on a sofa, busy with her sewing. It was usual for us to visit her in the drawing-room for an hour after tea, for which we had to change into different frocks. Occasionally she would play the piano and sing or whistle some tune for us, which we loved.

People seldom came to stay, except for Uncle Henry – Lord Henry Scott – my father's younger brother and our only surviving bachelor uncle. He was a keen horseman and was allowed to use Eildon as his headquarters during the hunting season. One of his cronies – Cospatrick Douglas-Home, great-uncle of Sir Alec, the former Prime Minister – was a regular visitor. Every year he used to take a nearby house for the season opposite the Buccleuch Arms in St. Boswells. St. Boswells was also where Uncle Henry stabled his hunters. Two days a week Uncle Henry and Cospatrick disappeared into Edinburgh to do something at a bank and thought themselves very hard worked; the rest of their time was spent hunting, shooting or fishing. Cospatrick always dropped in for lunch after he had been to church on Sundays. My father was a tease who got great pleasure from arguments and had no difficulty in getting Uncle Henry and Cospatrick thoroughly worked up. The talk was usually political and of no interest to my mother. She would sit in silence at one end of the table while the gentlemen argued away at the other. The last thing she would have done was join in the debate. I doubt if she so much as ticked off even the youngest of housemaids in the whole course of her life; she was too gentle and would not have known what to say. Occasionally some elderly female relation provided her with company for a few days, but on the whole I fear she must have had a lonely time.

[17]

Uncle Henry was a good friend to us children and played a part in encouraging us to ride. Sybil and I loved this more than anything. My father was not interested and my mother thought it dangerous, so outside encouragement was important to us. Luckily the Scotts in general were a hunting family. Uncle George Scott was Master of the Buccleuch Hunt at that date, and my brothers were also keen and helped us quite a lot. Walter, in time, was also to become Master of the Buccleuch. All this support no doubt insured that we soon had our own ponies. It was the custom for little girls to ride astride by then, but my mother did not think it nice for us to be seen in breeches so insisted that we wore thick divided skirts instead. These flapped about and could not have been more uncomfortable for the animals as well as ourselves. My mother much disliked our riding because she considered it dangerous, and yet we used to wear nothing on our heads other than floppy blue felt hats. At that time no one seemed to think it necessary for our heads to be protected. I frequently fell on mine but never seemed any the worse. We must have been a great worry for the groom in charge of us, however, as we always went as fast as we could and only stopped when the ponies themselves thought it was best to do so. Apart from the ponies and Jack Graham, our favourite groom, who – alas – did not return from the First World War, my earliest affections were bestowed upon my teddy bear; every evening I asked in my prayers that he might come to life. Later, however, these affections were transferred to the two foxhound puppies which were sent each year to be 'walked'. They lived in the stables and roamed the garden at large.

Being a large family we were inclined to pair off. Sybil was my main companion and guardian angel except, that is, when Billy came home for the holidays and she abandoned me for his older and more exciting company. I was only allowed to join them if I promised not to be tiresome or cry or go and hurt myself. We used to much enjoy the gardens at Eildon. Not only were there nice things to eat – lovely raspberries, peaches and figs – but the gardeners, with whom we were good friends, encouraged us to do our gardening by giving us plants. These we would cosset in our own little plots. One holiday Billy constructed a rock garden in the wood. The work absorbed us for hours on end. Its chief glory was a splendid pool, which grew more and more impressive as the days went by. It was, therefore, a particularly calamitous moment when an angry farmer correctly identified this centre-piece as the reason for a growing and previously inexplicable water shortage. Billy had diverted the local supply from his cows. Perhaps we found solace in walking down to the railway bridge and watching the trains, another Eildon treat.

From the age of six, in term time, we would be in the schoolroom and spend most of the day with the governess. We used to go through governesses at a tremendous rate, which is hardly surprising when one considers that my younger sister Mary – a beautiful, very strong child but with an all too easily aroused temper – once tried to push Miss Maffey, an immensely tall woman, out of the window. The exception was 'Meggie'. She was a wonderful teacher and a sweet person, from whom I learned much that was a great help in later years.

Meggie was also very religious, her father and brothers all being clergy, and insisted on morning prayers round the school-room table. When we were ready and kneeling she would ring a bell, at which signal the schoolroom footman would appear and have to join in. I am sure she did it purely for what she considered to be his own best interests, but it always filled me with embarrassment. Schoolroom lessons consisted of reading, writing and arithmetic and later German, French and sewing. Later on, Italian was added to the list.

From Eildon we would invariably go and stay with my grandparents at Drumlanrig Castle in Dumfriesshire. There, in the autumn, my grandfather liked to organise shooting parties for his sons and relatives. Of all our homes Drumlanrig was for me the most beautiful – and that includes the countryside surrounding it. A grass park studded with trees stretches away to the river Nith; and on the other three sides steep banks of mown grass lead down to flowerbeds cut in fantastic shapes, surrounded by clipped box hedges and gravel paths. Rising up and above acres of woodland with the wild moors beyond, it looks from a distance like a fairy castle.

Drumlanrig did not originally belong to the Scott family. It used to be the seat of the Red Douglases and the present house was built by a Douglas, the first Duke of Queensberry, at the end of the seventeenth century. Scotland, at that date, was only just emerging into the modern world of peace and organisation, the wars and bloodshed of the Middle Ages still a very present memory, and Drumlanrig as a result is an extraordinary cross between the civilised palace of a grandee and the defensive castle of a warrior chief. There are lovely sunny rooms looking out over the park and gardens and a tower at each of its four corners with dark and winding staircases. On calm evenings one went to sleep to the soothing sound of the Marr burn; but on stormy nights lay in fear as the winds howled and whistled round the turrets. The walls are built of pink granite and if there is sunshine after rain the flecks of mica in the stone make the whole Castle glitter like silver. Drumlanrig came into the Buccleuch family through the marriage of Francis, the second Duke, to Lady Jane Douglas, daughter of the second Duke of Queensberry. On the death of the last Duke of Queensberry in 1810 the title and property passed to the third Duke of Buccleuch, grandson of Lady Jane.

My grandfather loved to have children around and Sybil and I were the lucky ones chosen to be with him during his stay at Drumlanrig. The first time I went I must have been about eight. We stayed, accompanied by a governess and maid, from October till the move to Dalkeith House at Christmas. The day formally began with prayers in the chapel. The Reverend Mr Smith Dorian officiated, a retired parson who used to act as the private chaplain when my grandparents were in residence. These prayers were attended by Aunt Connie, Mr Whitmore (my grandfather's secretary), the housekeeper, housemaids and the children and governess. My grandparents and their guests only attended the Sunday service.

Later, after lessons, Sybil and I would joyfully set off on the morning ride. There were miles of beautifully kept grass rides

[20]

through the lovely woods and along the river bank. It must have taken many estate workmen to cut the sward and bracken and remove seedling trees. We could let our ponies go as fast as they wanted and when a ride divided, Sybil would go one way and I the other to the dismay of the groom who was there to look after us. Should he follow the elder girl on the spirited highbred pony or the younger one on the slower, more sedate animal? Luckily for him the rides usually coincided before we reached home. We loved galloping through those silent woods and past the small lochs, of which there were several. Wild duck would take off quacking loudly and often a roe deer or a red squirrel, which were quite numerous in those days, would cross our path. At one point there was also a large group of monkey-puzzle trees, some hundred or more years old, which used to interest us. We always hoped that one day we might see a monkey amongst them. Afternoons were left at our disposal and we would invent games and fight duels under the ancient yews below the Castle or, if the burn was in spate, watch the salmon and sea-trout leaping the waterfall.

It was a tradition that after tea the grown-ups would rush about with us in games of hide 'n seek or pounce piggy, a Scott variation in which two people hid and ambushed the rest. They seemed to enjoy it as much as we did and I expect some were quite glad of an opportunity to get into a dark cupboard or behind a thick curtain for a few secluded moments to themselves! The four towers of staircases and three floors of long passages gave plenty of exercise, and we must have run miles during the course of an evening. Our grandparents usually played each other at billiards after tea, and if they saw that we had nothing more exciting to do would often allow us to score for them. The task was not particularly exciting, but it had its compensations. When we scored patiently and correctly my grandfather would tip us a golden half-sovereign – something most acceptable since we were not given pocket money of any kind.

Probably five or six guests as well as members of the family would attend these parties and stay for a week or ten days. The men would go out pheasant and duck shooting – invariably supported by us and a rather unwilling Reverend Mr Smith Dorian. Drives around the countryside would be arranged for female guests and other non-combatants, or walks, including one to the kitchen garden, a mile away from the house, where there were over eight hundred yards of greenhouses to be strolled through and a summer house in which tea was sometimes held. If tea was in the Castle the ladies would have changed out of their heavy woollen day clothes and into lighter tea gowns. Then at 7.15, after their rampage with us, they would have been summoned to their rooms by the gong to bathe in the portable tubs prepared for them, and to change for dinner. Every lady brought a maid, every gentleman a valet. The dinner gong would be at 8.15.

Another sound that comes back to me is the gentle noise of the gravel being raked first thing in the mornings. This was carried out every day, whether the ground had been disturbed or not. Looking out one would see rows of old men raking away. The estate employed almost a hundred gardeners then. Many of them were of an age that nowadays would mean retirement and probable exile from the countryside altogether, but in those days they would all have had stone cottages on or near the estate and lived happy and contented working lives to the end. One of my favourite childhood books was called *Froggie's Little Brother*. It was about a slum boy and used to make me weep every time I read it; but my own experience of working people could not have been more different. Everybody was well looked after and their children were healthy and went to excellent village schools. In fact one of the things I should most like to convey of those times is how very, very nice all the servants (it hardly seems right to use such a word nowadays) were, and what real family friends. Indeed some of them were part of the family as far as we were concerned, having been connected with us for generations. Too often nowadays one is given the impression that all landowners were tyrants and their workers down-trodden serfs.

Nevertheless the servants, not least the domestic servants with whom we came into daily contact, formed a separate world with its own clearly defined system of rules and manners. 'Below stairs' there was a definite division: the steward's room, which was ruled by the house steward or butler and nicknamed the 'pugs' parlour' by the junior servants not privileged to enter it – and the general meeting place of the servants' hall. Status was clearly defined. The head of the household was the steward, who controlled everything and everybody, from the setting of the clocks to the travelling arrangements of the guests; from the dismissal of the staff to the organisation and restocking of the cellars. Next to the steward in rank was the housekeeper, who looked after the arrangements of the lady guests and controlled the female staff. Then came the groom-of-the-chambers, who saw to the particular welfare of the guests. It was part of his responsibility to check that the writing tables were neat and in order – every pencil sharpened, every pen polished and ink-well full each morning – and that the flowers in the house were fresh and trim. Finally there was the under-butler, the junior member of the dominating triumvirate of the male staff, who was in charge of the silver and the footmen, probably numbering at least three.

The housemaids rose between 5 and 6 a.m. to sweep all the fireplaces and rooms before 9 a.m. after which they had to be as invisible as possible in their duties. Carpets would all have been brushed with a broom and the grates polished – least popular of household chores. The groom-of-the-chambers would supervise the gardeners, if the flowers were being restocked, and the odd-man would scurry to and fro with baskets of logs. Later there would be the valeting to attend to, bells to be answered and the dining-room to prepare for the gentlemens' breakfast. Ladies breakfasted in bed. At some point the steward would pass by to make sure everything was in order. Meanwhile, from 6 a.m. the kitchenmaids and stillroom maids were busy preparing the various breakfasts for the dining room, schoolroom, nursery, individual guests, steward's room and servants' hall. Even in this a considerable etiquette had to be observed. The stillroom maid was required to cook all the boiled eggs, except for the guests breakfasting in the dining room, but no other kind. Fried eggs, poached, scrambled and the rest were done in the kitchen. Nor, once the egg was boiled, did the stillroom maid play any further part in its life. It then became the responsibility of another maid, who took it to the kitchen where the trays were prepared, before bearing it aloft to the appointed bedroom. No wonder, when news reached the nursery on one occasion that the second nurse was engaged to the groom-of-the-chambers, the housekeeper was heard to exclaim to the nanny: 'Where ever can they have met?'

Of course stillroom and kitchenmaids had many other duties. Everything to do with tea emanated from the stillroom and every day after lunch the kitchenmaids scrubbed the floors of the kitchen, scullery and all the larders, spreading fresh sawdust where necessary. The heavier job of cleaning the long basement passage was undertaken once a week by odd-job men using deck scrubbers.

There was said to be a ghost at Drumlanrig. My mother saw it as a young girl on her first visit to the house. She and her sister, the two beautiful Miss Bridgemans, were sent there – presumably thanks to the scheming of their mother and the Duchess of Buccleuch – in the hope that one of them would catch my father's eye. On their way to bed, the candle flames no doubt faltering from time to time in the draught of the passage, they saw something furry moving towards them. They were terrified. The candle blew out, but luckily they found the door of their bedroom, rushed in and, after their excited report at the time, never much liked to talk about it again. Then, years later, after my mother had indeed become the Countess of Dalkeith, she was found in the hall looking pea-green by one of her guests, Lady Mabel Howard. 'What's the matter with you!' exclaimed Lady Mabel. 'It's the most extraordinary thing,' replied my mother. 'I saw a huge monkey sitting on the chair there.' 'My dear, are you feeling quite well? You haven't had too much for lunch?' asked Lady Mabel; but no, my mother repeated that it was just the result of seeing the monkey and, as on the first occasion with her sister, insisted that nothing further should be made of it. Shortly afterwards, during the First World War, Drumlanrig was turned into a hospital. One day the matron asked our agent's wife, who was running things, if she could speak to her on a matter of urgency. 'I saw something awful in the night,' she said as soon as they were alone, 'and I'm afraid I just can't stay.' 'What did you see?' 'I wouldn't like to say,' said the matron. 'I don't think the family would like it. But I must go. I can't stay.' So she left, and nobody knew why; but after the War someone was looking through the books in the muniment room and they came on an inventory for the house in 1700. The matron's room was called 'Yellow Monkey or Haunted Room'.

My only unpleasant memory of Drumlanrig is of having diphtheria there – a frightening disease which they presumed I must have contracted on the train journey, since no one else around was known to have had it (injections against it were unknown in those days). A little girl in a long frock came to talk to me and I was somewhat mystified because her feet were three or four inches off the floor. No doubt I was delirious, but it would not surprise me if she really was the ghost of some child who had lived in that room generations before – her hovering perhaps explained by the floor having sunk since that distant time. Otherwise my most lasting memory of the Castle in those pre-First World War days is of Sybil. Thinking me inside the lavatory she is saying 'I can see you but you can't see me' at the door when to her horror, whom should emerge but . . . the Reverend Mr Smith Dorian!

Annual visits came to an end in 1913, and during the First World War Drumlanrig became a hospital. It was not until 1927 that the family returned to a house transformed by the introduction of electric lighting, bathrooms and every modern convenience.

3

DECEMBER FOUND US on the move again, this time to Dalkeith House on the outskirts of the town of Dalkeith near Edinburgh. Here the whole family used to assemble annually for Christmas and the New Year; so it was at Dalkeith that I celebrated all the Christmas Day birthdays of my childhood. The house, except for an estate office, was closed on the death of my grandfather in 1914 and has never been occupied by any member of the family since that date. Its treasures were eventually distributed among the other Buccleuch homes and its rooms let out as offices and flats.

Dalkeith, like Drumlanrig, was originally a Douglas stronghold. It had changed hands several times in the course of its history, including a period in the fifteenth century when it acted as the notorious 'Lion's Den' of the Regent Morton; so its stones, though partially reorganized to form an eighteenth-century mansion, had witnessed plenty of dark and bloody deeds over the years.

The property was bought by the Buccleuchs in the middle of the seventeenth century, a troublesome enough period in itself. General Monk used the house as his headquarters in Scotland during the Commonwealth and is said to have planned the restoration of Charles II from here. The latter, on regaining the throne, married his eldest son – James, Duke of Monmouth – to the Countess Anna Buccleuch. Monmouth was also declared the first Duke of Buccleuch, but the title of Duchess was conferred on Anna in her own right three years later, thus saving her title and lands from being attainted when Monmouth was later disgraced and executed for rebelling against his uncle James II. The eldest son of Monmouth and Duchess Anna did not outlive his mother, so it was the grandson of the marriage who became the second Duke.

Perhaps it was a murky happening in the distant past of the house that accounted for the spooky spot between the double doors leading into the upstairs drawing room. Sybil and I had to pass there on the way to our mother's sitting room, and always found it an ordeal. We used to hold hands, shut our eyes and run through as fast as possible. Many years later one of my uncles told me that he had felt the same. That was not the only frightening aspect of the place. Some of the walls were very deep and the lavatory we used was set into one of these. It was dark and eerie with only one small window for light, high up. We dreaded the door being closed and the possibility of getting locked in. One of the bedrooms had a brass plate on the door inscribed with the name of General Monk; and after the War, when the old cellars were cleared out, eighteen venerable bottles were discovered with a label proclaiming them to be 'General Monck's Amontillado'. Rowland, the steward, reported this discovery to my father, whose only response was: 'No such wine ever existed.'

Our journey to Dalkeith was by special train hired to convey the family, servants, carriages, horses, ponies and a vast amount of luggage from Drumlanrig. The Hampdens and other cousins would arrive in due course to swell the numbers. The house was referred to as the 'Palace' by the local townspeople, and contained a great many large rooms with high ceilings and carved doors. The little entrance hall was dominated by a huge painting of a Moorish giant. We lived in dread of him coming suddenly to life. Beyond lay a long friendlier hall with a large table running down the middle, covered in tweed coats and capes, mackintoshes, hats, sticks, umbrellas and, more often than not, with one or two patient labradors sprawled underneath. Against one wall stood a splendid weighing machine, with a comfortable green leather seat and a place on which to put an array of weights, ranging from four stone down to the odd ounce. It was a house rule that every guest be weighed when they left and the result written in a 'Visitors' Book'. Usually facetious comments followed the entries, like 'After lunch!' or 'Go easy on the pudding next time!' Unfortunate guests of the Buccleuchs had to undergo the same torture at Bowhill, the family's residence in the Borders and the house that was later to fulfill the Christmas role of Dalkeith. We loved using the machine, going up and down till the correct number of weights was placed on the opposite side.

The hall was where we congregated for church, the private chapel at Dalkeith being in the park and also serving as the town's Episcopalian church. When at Bowhill or Langholm we sometimes used to attend the kirk so as to offset this preference and show there was no ill-feeling. My mother always professed to be religious but not my father. He attended on Sundays because he felt he ought to, but wound his watch threateningly if the sermon was taking too long. We would complete the poor clergyman's discomfort by running our dormice along the pews. Religion was by no means forced down our throats. In fact it was Sybil who taught me 'The Lord's Prayer'. This was when I was about four. Up till then I could only recite 'Gentle Jesus, meek and mild', which I did not like at all. 'Pity my simplicity', in particular, I found nonsensical and hard to say. Learning 'The Lord's Prayer' came as a great relief. It seemed a very grown-up thing to be able to do.

With no electricity the only light was from candles, the odd gas lamp and fires – which, of course, were almost the sole source of heat. In the night nursery we used to go to bed with a raging log fire and I loved watching the flickering light of its flames on the walls and ceilings. I shared the room with Sybil and a nursery maid. One evening I awoke to whispers and peeping over the sheet was much intrigued to see the nursery maid drying the footman's hair at the fireside. Footmen powdered their hair before waiting at dinner and were expected to have every trace of it brushed or washed out by the time they reported for duty the following morning. I suspect there was neither hot water nor a warm fire to dry by in the footmens' quarters and our nursery maid's friend was luckier than the others, though no doubt he would have got in a lot of trouble if he had been caught. Powder was an economy, wigs being more expensive and reserved only for coachmen.

Up in the attics were several enormous trunks full of old clothes: uniforms, crinolines, men's silk embroidered waistcoats and satin pages' suits of pink and pale blue in a wide variety of sizes. The suits had most probably been made for Coronations, but in common with many of the clothes may have been much older. There were also a lot of smelly old wigs. The clothes stank no less pungently of mothballs, but we loved dressing up in them nonetheless. The grown-ups used them as well, donning them every year for a grand Christmas fancy-dress dinner. This traditionally followed a fancy-dress tea for the children. In later years the custom was carried on at Bowhill. It was there that our cousin Miss Lucy Hope once appeared as a geisha girl. She was a formidable, middle-aged lady with a pronounced moustache and to everyone's horror Billy, the self-appointed master of ceremonies, announced that she had won first prize for coming as an Afghan chief!

When I was five or six I was particularly devoted to my cousin David Brand (later Lord Hampden). One day Billy took us aside: 'If you go to the summer-house in the old wood you'll find a fairy there who'll marry you and let you live happily ever after on Scotch broth and chocolate meringues,' he confided earnestly. The wood was the remains of the old Caledonian forest of ancient oak trees, a fairy-tale place for all us children, and at its centre stood an attractive Victorian summer-house, its walls lined with a layer of dry heather and an intricate pattern of fir cones and nuts. David and I followed Billy's instructions and after a prolonged vigil in the hut, during which no fairy appeared, became both disillusioned and frightened. Meanwhile the alarm had been raised: frantic nannies chased everywhere, the river bank was scoured. Eventually Billy was asked where he had last seen us and, following his disclosures, we were rescued.

At one point the river bank was riddled with an eccentric

assortment of artificial caves made in Victorian times, one of them longer than the others and dark in the centre. Here we played horrific games of pirates. 'Beetle juice' was head of the pirates and also had a hide-out in the house, a small, dark room at the bottom of a winding stair, where the footmen cleaned the lamps. Before I was old enough to be enlisted as a pirate I was allowed to go and visit this awesome figure, escorted by Sybil. It was quite a while before I discovered that the dreaded 'Beetle juice' was Billy.

There were plenty of other amusements. In a wide passage on the first floor was a huge grey rocking-horse belonging to the previous generation of young Scotts. Three of us could fit on its back and one on each of its rockers. Nearby there was a very special grandfather clock. When it struck the hour a row of little soldiers marched past just below the face. The clock is now on public display at Bowhill. So is another curiosity from Dalkeith: a large glass case containing a musical box in which, at the turn of a handle, three monkeys in eighteenth-century dress do conjuring tricks on a table with some dice.

Aunt Connie, to whom we were devoted, was a great organizer of games and treats. Before the estate Christmas party she always produced a deep bowl filled with different coloured fruit-drops and these we would scoop, stir energetically and shovel into bags and baskets to hang on the Christmas tree. I always found it rather hard having my birthday on Christmas Day, but it certainly never lessened the excitement and sometimes even had compensations. It enabled me, for instance, to join Aunt Connie on the annual trip to the pantomime in Edinburgh. She referred to it in a letter to me written not long before she died:

> 'I often think of our pantomime parties from Dalkeith. Mr Whitmore of the party, as he had charge of the tickets – but why did Canon Cooke go also? Surely a most unsuitable person for a pantomime! I always had charge of the youngest allowed to go, and remember you were allowed to go at an earlier age than others, because of your Christmas birthday. I remember you slept soundly

[30]

in my arms all the way home in the family bus, and you were quite heavy – but I did not mind as I loved you very much.'

The 'family bus' was a horse drawn waggonette, sitting five people aside facing each other.

The policies at Dalkeith stood between the North and South Esk. Along the banks were well-kept gravel paths where nannies were apt to take prams and children the day before a duck shoot, causing considerable annoyance to the guns who found all the ducks had flown elsewhere by the appointed time. The head keeper was a splendid fellow called Mr Chowler, who rode about wearing a square bowler hat. He was a great expert on the Stock Exchange and visiting guns would buttonhole him throughout the day on the subject of their portfolios. Apparently when he died he left several thousand pounds, a lot of money at that time.

One of the most frequent guests from outside the family, and certainly our favourite, was my grandfather's friend Lord Rosebery, the former Prime Minister and the last holder of that office to own a winner of the Derby. He enjoyed joking with and teasing us children, and Mary called him 'Lord Strawberry', because of his red nose. In her day Queen Victoria often stayed at Dalkeith, preferring it to Holyrood when she visited Edinburgh.

In 1911 my youngest brother George was born in the house just before a visit by King George and Queen Mary. My mother asked the Queen if she would honour the baby by being a godmother, to which she said she would be delighted but forgot to mention it to the King. The following day the King said to my father that he would like to be the baby's godfather. My father and mother did not dare mention about Queen Mary and gratefully accepted.

The festivities at Dalkeith over, we once again boarded a hired train, just like a circus on the move, and headed for Bowhill at the heart of the Scott country in the Borders. The estate lies within the boundaries of the ancient Ettrick Forest – at one time the favourite hunting grounds of the Kings of Scotland. Various Scotts were rangers there in the Middle Ages and, according to legend, it was the courage of a certain young Scott when saving the King's hounds from a ferocious buck deep in a forest 'cleuch' or ravine, that earned the family their titular name of Buccleuch (Buck-Cleuch). No part of the eighteenth-century building is visible today, the house having been rebuilt and successively added to during the first half of the nineteenth century.

The new Bowhill was the house most associated with Sir Walter Scott. Scott was a kinsman of the family, befriended at an early stage of his career by the third Duke and in his prime by the fourth. Writing in old age of the young fifth Duke he observed that 'I would not have him quite so soft natured as his grandfather, whose kindness sometimes mastered his excellent understanding. His father had a temper which better jumped with my humour. Enough of ill nature to keep your good nature from being abused is no bad ingredient in their disposition who have favours to bestow.' The fifth Duke proved the match of any that had preceded him, a distinguished public servant and generous private benefactor, who was acknowledged as one of the most enlightened and successful landowners of his time. It was this Duke's mother who gave Scott the idea for his first great literary success 'The Lay of the Last Minstrel' and the poem was dedicated to his father, Duke Charles. The minstrel begins his lay at Newark Castle, a ruin two miles north of the house, and in one stanza refers to the enchantments of 'sweet Bowhill'.

This is an apt description. Though the house is not beautiful or even particularly distinguished, it was always the happiest and most comfortable of our homes and placed in a particularly beautiful situation between the fast flowing rivers of Ettrick and Yarrow. In the park and just visible from the windows are two lakes which frequently froze solid in winter, providing a chance for the young to play violent games of ice-hockey, and the elderly the more restful sport of curling – their calls of 'Soop! Soop! Soop!' echoing as they agitatedly brushed the ice clean before their gliding stones.

In time for Easter, the family would move south again to pass the summer at Boughton, in Northamptonshire. My grandfather handed over this property to my father early in the

Family group 1902: *(left to right)* Walter, Sybil, Mother, self, Billy and 'Mida' (Margaret Ida).

Drumlanrig, Dumfries-shire: The family's autumn residence
and loveliest of all the Buccleuch houses.

Boughton, Northamptonshire: My parents' summer home –
half palace, half village.

century; and here, as children, we stayed every year from Easter till the middle of June, when we left for our few weeks as guests of our grandparents at Montagu House.

Boughton, like Montagu House, was originally the property of the Montagu family and became a portion of the Buccleuch estates only when Duke Henry, the third Duke, married the Montagu heiress in the middle of the eighteenth century. The architecture of the house documents the occupations and fortunes of its owners in a remarkable way, from its origins as a monastery, through the homely additions by the knightly Montagus of Elizabethan times, to the Versailles-like facade imposed by the first Duke at the end of the seventeenth century and expressly designed to be fit for a king – he hoped it would tempt William and Mary to come and stay, and thus keep him as much in favour with the protestant Orange court as the catholic Stuart one it had replaced. It is, in other words, not one building but a hotch-potch of buildings – its palatial front hiding a positive village of houses and courtyards of varying date, best revealed by an aerial view.

But it is Ralph, the first Duke, and John, the second, who have most left their mark. Ralph was in fact born only the second son, but his elder brother disgraced himself at Charles II's court by 'squeezing the Queen's hand', and Ralph took his place. In due course he rose to a dukedom and the post of ambassador at the court of Louis XIV, which experience led him to build this magnificent French chateau in the heart of the English countryside. The great north front and many of the treasures in the Buccleuch collections are his legacy; the park is that of his son, John. The latter wanted to have an avenue of trees from Boughton to old Montagu House in Bloomsbury, but was unable to arrange this with the landowners en route. Instead he planted his seventy miles-worth of trees in avenues encircling and crisscrossing the estate. Between 1750 and 1900 the house was unused and therefore escaped change to an unusual degree. The only aspect to suffer was Duke John's elaborate system of canals, lakes and fountains in the park. These have now been dug out and repaired at the instigation of my nephew Johnnie, the present

[33]

Duke, so that the vistas, enlivened by water effects, are now largely restored to their eighteenth-century glory.

Boughton always reminds me of cuckoos and the cawing of the rooks in the spring; summer days, warm and peaceful, with cotton frocks (such things as woollen cardigans did not exist then) and wildflowers – bluebells, fritillaries in profusion. We were allowed to roam at large, nobody seeming to worry that we might drown in the lily-pond or the river running through the park. We loved the birds and chasing the butterflies. We loved Boughton – but because it was English we could never admit to it.

Four villages stand at the edge of the park, each a mile or so distant from the house, and on Sundays their intermingling church bells made a lovely sound. From each of them, on May 1, would come in turn separate groups of children, the girls garlanded and the boys holding bunches of spring flowers as they carried their May Queen on a throne smothered in blooms and leafy branches. After singing songs they would dance around the maypole and then, to the delight of all, we showered them with well-polished pennies, thrown as far as possible to cause the greatest chase and scramble.

When it was too wet to be out-of-doors we took ourselves off to the top floor of the house, where endless unoccupied attics were perfect for hide 'n seek. Hardly anyone had been up there for 150 years, and in one room there was a very large and ancient billiard table (revered today as one of the oldest in England), upon which we played many exciting games of our own invention. It was a dusty and mysterious place, and we were forever alert to the possible excitement of meeting the mad Montagu duchess who, it was said, had been locked up in one of the rooms generations before. She, so the story went, had been a lady of great wealth and equal eccentricity, who declared that the only man she could possibly marry was the Emperor of China. The cunning Duke of Montagu therefore dressed up as the Emperor when he went to ask for her hand in marriage, which of course she bestowed with glee. Then, as soon as the marriage was completed and her wealth was his, he locked her up in the attic.

The panelled attic walls were painted a pale grey and were full of mice and bats. Bats were a great feature of Boughton. Once, in our absence, some strange noises in my father's sitting room were investigated, and as a result three hundred dead ones were removed from behind a strip of panelling. Our nursery was a long gallery with a large carved wooden fireplace in the centre of one wall, and our schoolroom a beautiful library of leather-bound books and oak panelling. Most of the rooms in the house were hung with tapestries, one of the Dukes of Montagu having owned the Mortlake factory. To children these could be very frightening, as they depicted classical scenes with gruesome animals or violent episodes from the Bible. In a draught they would move gently, which could be alarming in the twilight, and they filled the whole building with a mysterious, peppery odour. Not long ago some rather naughty drawings and remarks were discovered chalked on the wall behind a tapestry in one of the bedrooms. They were the work, apparently, of Sybil and me as children.

The house was cluttered with treasures, but we were never told to be careful of them or anything like that. They were just taken for granted. No curator cared for them, no parties of connoisseurs came to visit, and my parents were basically uninterested by possessions. My father, it is true, much concerned himself with the pictures, but only in the sense that he liked to see them arranged strictly in accordance with their size. He spent hours with his valet rehanging the collection, but when it came to furniture preferred to sit in the comfort of an old garden wicker chair to anything more elegant. As for sculpture, he and my uncles spent their youth trying to knock the noses off the statues of their Montagu ancestors with cricket balls. The statues stood along a colonnade by the front door, high off the ground, so hitting them accurately was quite a test; nevertheless every nose had gone by the time I arrived.

In a distant part of the house lived my Great Aunt Ada, widow of Admiral Lord Charles Scott, captain of the ship in which my father had served as a midshipman. She was a splendid old lady, greatly loved by us all and particularly by my mother. One of her

[35]

sons, a land agent, lived with her. He had the unique distinction of owning a motorbike with a wicker side-car and, as a special treat, would sometimes allow Sybil, then about thirteen, to ride it and me, aged eleven, to accompany her as the passenger. He and his brother (Sir David Scott, now in his ninety-sixth year, who still lives there) flew hawks, which they kept on hoops on the lawn. The hawks had to be fed on live mice and were frequently released to catch little birds. We thought it very cruel, but dearly loved these grown-up cousins nonetheless. Another of our favourites was Great Aunt Ada's niece, Maie Ryan, who occasionally appeared from Australia. Her future husband was to become Lord Casey, Governor of Bengal and later Governor-General of Australia. She was always spirited and entertaining and today, at the age of ninety, still flies her own aeroplane.

The summer of 1914 found my eldest sister 'Mida' grown up, Walter (Lord Whitchester) at Oxford and Billy at Sandhurst. At Montagu House there were dinner parties for the young and Mida's coming-out ball. Sybil and I would leave our beds and peer out of the window to watch the assembled guests sitting or walking about on the terrace below. Occasionally we would shout a rude remark to some special friend or drop a message or vulgar drawing. Now and again Walter arrived in the school-room with a party of Oxford friends, pillow fights and much teasing and ragging being the inevitable result. More often than not he would be accompanied by 'Bobbity' Cranborne (the late Lord Salisbury), Mike and Rose Bowes-Lyon (brother and elder sister of the Queen Mother), Prince Paul of Serbia and a young German, Count von Beiberstein. The schoolroom would be left in chaos, our governess (few of whom lasted more than a year, not surprisingly) having tactfully withdrawn. World War I was about to break out, irrevocably changing the lives of us all.

My grandfather outlived my grandmother by two years and died that first autumn of the War. He was buried at Dalkeith. When we heard we were going to the funeral we felt grand and grown-up but also terrified that we might see his corpse. This we were spared, but on the day I was no less horrified by the sight of the coffin being lowered into the vault. I do not think children should be made to attend funerals. Afterwards a period of mourning was observed during which we were all plunged into black, even to the buttons on the footmens' livery.

4

MY FATHER, being the second son, had never expected to succeed to the title. He was educated at the Royal Naval College, Dartmouth and, I have been told, was destined for a brilliant career in the Navy had his elder brother not unexpectedly died. At the age of twelve as a midshipman he went to Australia and the Far East in the *Bacchante*, commanded by my great uncle, Lord Charles Scott. Also on board as naval cadets were the two sons of the Prince of Wales – the Duke of Clarence and Prince George, the latter in time to succeed his father as George V. They were accompanied by their tutor, Mr Dalton. As a result of this trip King George and my father remained always the best of friends. Mr Dalton afterwards submitted an exhaustive report on the voyage to Queen Victoria and the Prince and Princess of Wales, which does not describe anything too hazardous as having taken place. It also fails to mention the incident when my great-uncle Charles assembled the ship's company before docking at Sydney, and warned them about the many attractive girls they might find there and the importance of not succumbing to their charms. Before the ship left for home, he himself fell in love with, and subsequently married, my Australian aunt Ada Ryan! News of the match was received with horror, but my family need not have worried: Aunt Ada proved, as I have already indicated, a great addition. She was a charming and delightful person and lived to be ninety-five, loved by us all.

My father was still only in his early twenties when in 1886 his elder brother slipped on a wet rock at Achnacarry while stalking. His rifle went off and the bullet pierced an artery in his arm. He bled to death on the long trail home. As a result my father had to leave the Navy, much to his sorrow, and return home to the responsibilities of a son and heir. In due course, also, to think about marrying. I suspect my two grandmothers busily made plans on his behalf. They were both members of the Court – my father's mother, the Duchess of Buccleuch being Mistress of the Robes to Queen Alexandra; my mother's mother, the Countess of Bradford, Lady-in-Waiting to the future Queen Mary, then Duchess of York. They knew each other well and were the best of friends. Soon two Bradford daughters barely out of the schoolroom, the beautiful Lady Beatrice and Lady Margaret Bridgeman, were despatched to Drumlanrig.

I feel sorry for my mother. It is difficult to imagine anyone less well prepared for marriage than she must have been, after her secluded upbringing at her country home in Shropshire. Her father, by all accounts, was inconsiderately mean towards his family and interested only in racing and his own health – for the benefit of which he made frequent visits to the spas and resorts made fashionable by the Prince of Wales, leaving my grandmother with virtually no money and six children to bring up.

To us 'Guida' (short for Granny Ida) always seemed rather serious and reserved, even something of a 'goody goody', but my husband told me that in his childhood 'Ida B', as they called her, had been a great favourite with him and his brothers and sister, very much the life and soul of the party. This is well illustrated by the fact that she was the first person to fly with the Prince of Wales after he received his licence, though she must have been in her eighties at the time.

My other grandmother, Louisa, Duchess of Buccleuch, was also greatly loved and much respected at Court. She had a host of friends as well as a large family to entertain, something she thoroughly enjoyed. A daughter of the Duke and Duchess of Abercorn, she was the eldest in a family of thirteen, which enabled my father to have two uncles younger than himself. At a lunch party at Barnwell when my son William was about six years old, the conversation turned to the subject of large and small families. I casually remarked that my grandmother was one of thirteen. I saw William looking horrified and when the guests had left he asked me if what I had said was really true. 'Of course,' I replied. 'But how dreadful!' he exclaimed. 'Did they have to drown some?' The labrador had just had a litter of eleven pups, five of which had had to be drowned, doubtless causing him much distress and now some confusion.

I do not know how long my parents' courtship lasted – they were both very shy so it may have taken some while. My mother told me that one Sunday, when my father was staying at her home, Weston, Guida told her firmly: 'You're starting a cold. You'd better not come to Church.' Mamma, always meek and mild, agreed, though she had not the slightest symptom of a cold. My father then said: 'Oh well, I'll stay and keep you company.' By the time the church party returned they were engaged.

In due course they got married. It was brave of my mother to accept the proposal. She was only eighteen, and for someone who had never been away from home it must have been quite alarming to join such a large and boisterous family. As it was, I do not think she ever really blossomed. My father always liked noisy, cheerful people; but my mother found it difficult to compete with social gatherings. We did not see much of her but when we did she nearly always seemed to be lying on the sofa or on a long-chair in the garden. When my father invited his noisy ladies to stay – Lady Mabel Howard, who never stopped talking, or our Aunt Celia Scarbrough – she generally disappeared to bed with a 'headache'. Her main interest was in her babies, with the boys always her favourites. Having babies also gave her an excuse, I am sure, to get away from everyone: this enormous, tiresome, family of quarrelsome Scotts; her noisy brood of little girls driving her mad! Her favourite child was my youngest brother, George, who was a dear little boy. She doted on him, but luckily he grew up none the worse for this.

Her somewhat inadequate education had been shared with three sisters and given by an elderly governess. She had little idea

[40]

of how to run a house or who was supposed to do what, so left everything to the housekeeper. Housemaids living in freezing cold rooms in the attics – that sort of thing – simply did not concern her. My sister-in-law Rachel Scott remembers her visiting Bowhill towards the end of her life and being excited to discover it had a basement! Where she imagined the food had been cooked one cannot imagine. And yet she would often make us take the remains of the roly-poly pudding, or something equally unsuitable, to old ladies in cottages on the estate who probably did not want it a bit. I always felt sorry for her, even when I was a child. My father seemed continually to be away at that time, and she can scarcely have known anyone outside her family before marrying him. The visits she made with us children to Hyde Park, wearing the extraordinary hats she made herself, sitting on uncomfortable tin chairs, attended by her collection of funny old gentlemen, seem, in retrospect, all the more pathetic and sad. She must often have suffered from loneliness.

My father also hated formal events, but was sociable enough in his own house. He enjoyed arguments and political and historical discussion, voluble men and talkative ladies. He was never at a loss for a word and usually the winner of any argument, but was kindness itself beneath it all. His great passion was for trees and forestry, a subject on which he was well informed. What he most despised was any kind of pretension. Asked to open some event at the New Club in Edinburgh, he agreed only when he was convinced that there would be no pompous ceremony involved. Arriving in Princes Street on the day, however, he spied from a distance that the Lord Provost and city fathers were all dressed to the nines and lined up outside the building waiting for him. So he told his chauffeur to stop the Rolls Royce at the tram stop, got out and, to the astonishment of the dignitaries, arrived at the Club stepping off the tram. He disliked his tea being too hot, and at 'functions' caused some surprise by sloshing it from the cup to the saucer and back again; no doubt quietly amused by the horrified expressions as people agonised over whether or not to follow the ducal example. At home the valet would pour my father's tea about five minutes before he appeared for nine o'clock breakfast. Nervous young men would come down, see this cup waiting to be drunk, and think, 'I suppose I'd better take it'; only to be mortified a few minutes later by my father furiously demanding to know where his tea had gone.

Breakfast was also the cause of a rift between my father and Lord Frederick Hamilton, one of his two uncles younger than himself. Getting to the dining-room rather punctually one morning, Uncle Freddie devoured my father's boiled egg as well as his own. As this took place in the middle of the War at a time of considerable food shortages, one egg represented a fair proportion of the official weekly ration. My father was furious and banned him from the house forthwith. But Uncle Freddie was too much of a favourite of us all for the order to hold for more than a week or two. Full of fun and jokes, he usually arrived in a silly disguise of some sort and proceeded to annoy my mother by telling jokes at mealtime – usually rather vulgar ones in a loud voice, making the footmen giggle.

After the War my father's dining-room troubles were still not at an end. He was particularly pained by the way Lady Victoria Manners hacked the ham, and it became the custom to hide it during her visit. At Langholm the place chosen was under the typewriter cover in the secretary's room next to the dining room. That poor lady must have had some awful shocks as she settled to the afternoon's work!

The War ended and meals returned to their pre-war scale. At breakfast, apart from the array of dishes on the hot-plate of porridge, eggs and bacon, kidneys, sausages, mushrooms and tomatoes, there would be a ham, a tongue and, in the appropriate season, a choice of cold game. On top of lunch and tea, there were enormous dinners of soup, fish, entrée, roast, sweet, savoury, cheese and fruit with a different wine for every course. Rowland, who joined the staff as schoolroom footman in 1915, remembers a good deal of entertaining going on even during the War. He soon rose to the rank of butler and later on, steward. According to his account the total staff at the new London house, 2 Grosvenor Place, consisted of a steward, housekeeper, valet, under-butler, two parlour maids, five housemaids, cook, three kitchenmaids, two stillroom maids, two ladies' maids, two oddmen, carpenter, steward's room boy, two nurses, head coachmen, second coachman, carriage groom, three stablemen and a chauffeur. Breakfast in the steward's room was regularly composed of beer and cold mutton. Doubtless more than half the food sent to the dining room returned uneaten downstairs to the benefit of those below.

Miss Barford was our governess when the news was broken that Sybil and I were to be sent away to boarding school. This came as quite a shock. I was twelve and a half, Sybil fifteen. Mary, Angela and George were in or about to come into the schoolroom, and I suppose if we had stayed at home it would have meant the cost of a second governess. Heathfield was the most fashionable school of the time and the one to which my mother had originally thought of sending us; but when she saw what she considered to be the unnecessary and unsuitable lavishness of its clothes list – white silk frocks, white silk stockings, white satin pumps for dancing class – she dismissed it as a possibility. St James's, in contrast, called only for white cotton shirts and navy blue coats and skirts.

The school was at West Malvern, Worcestershire – an unusual Victorian house built by Lord Howard de Walden on the slopes of the Malvern Hills. There was a lovely view and the school was surrounded by beautiful grounds and gardens, tended by a school of lady gardeners. Miss Alice Baird had charge of the Senior House and Miss Diana Baird, her sister, of the Junior House of eleven to fourteen-year-olds. The Miss Bairds were remarkable: five spinster sisters all over six feet tall and all to be Head Mistresses.

Our journey to school was for us a great adventure. We travelled alone, usually breaking the journey to stay a night with our grandmother, 'Guida', at Castle Bromwich – an Elizabethan manor that still stands, but is now lost in one of the busiest areas of Birmingham. Then it was surrounded by beautiful gardens stretching away to a golf course and small aerodrome. Although I was under age I was allowed to join the Senior School at St

[43]

James's, so as to share a sister's room with Sybil. Four little rooms were set aside for this purpose at the far end of the house, necessitating a lot of running to and from the main scene of events, but having the advantage of being distant from all its noise and clatter. The Miss Bairds did their best to make school life as pleasant as possible, but nevertheless it was something of a shock and contrast to the comforts of home. The position of the house was exposed and it could be bitterly cold, especially in our bedroom annexe, with its three outside walls and windows to the floor. Even in winter these windows had to be opened at night and sometimes we would wake to find snow on the floor. It was cold in the classrooms, too, because of the war-time shortages of fuel; and the quality of the food was equally affected. Main meals seemed to consist of nothing but rissoles, and I broke a tooth on a nail in my porridge. My brothers were even worse off at the Front. They wrote continually about food. A letter from Billy in the summer of 1915 is typical.

Dear Alice,
You might let my father know that several articles arrived safely, viz, 1 Fowl in tin; 2 tins of sardines; 3 tins of herrings; 1 tin of rolled ox tongue; many tins of cream cocoa etc, also such items as Dubbin.
We live entirely on the tinned stuff from England as the only meat out here is pork and the ration beef is not very tempting.
The asparagus is very good: but the best of all was the fowl in a tin.
What I particularly want is a tinned ham, or a big corned beef to have as a midday meal, and some *salad oil* or *mayonnaise sauce* would be very useful.
Cakes are also very useful. In fact send the same as now only more.
We have had a quiet time in the trenches with only a few casualties.
I am only about 12–16 miles from Walter but cannot arrange to see him.
Love from Billy.

[44]

Letters were a rarity in the last War, everything being so heavily censored, whereas in the First War everything was quite open. After lunch Miss Baird would read us newspaper reports of the fighting. The death-lists, which covered all ranks, were a daily horror, but nevertheless we were not unduly anxious. It all seemed so far away from St James's. My parents never wrote and no relatives came to visit us during our time there – we were more than thankful, for we felt sure they would have disgraced us by saying or doing 'the wrong thing'!

Being philosophical, we realised we had to be at school, so had better make the most of it and enjoy everything there was to enjoy. I was soon enrolled as a Girl Guide, which I took very seriously, continuing my connection with the Movement for many years after. I also greatly enjoyed the games and had no difficulty with the lessons. On arrival I had been placed in a class of girls a year older than myself, but never found any trouble keeping up. There were no 'O Levels' or 'A Levels' in those days, and exams were not taken seriously. 'Citizenship' was what the Miss Bairds were most anxious to instill; it must be admitted with considerable success – many girls were later notable for lives of public service. In my time there were about eighty pupils, but I did not make any great friends. People never seem to do so at school. To add to the enjoyment of our train journeys Sybil and I used to take a little cardboard box with a hole in it; when anyone opened the door to come into the carriage one of us would say nervously to the other: 'I do hope the bees don't escape!' We also had some terrible black masks which we put on with our scarves tied round. I think my cousin Charles Scott meant to be sarcastic when he wrote a poem for our family magazine about what a goody-goody I was. It began:

> 'Alice was really a good little girl
> who loved to go to school.
>   The five Miss Bairds called her their pearl
> For never she broke a rule.
> A model was she for all the rest
> And every day she did her best.'

Not so complimentary was a ruthless rhyme by Lord Ernest Hamilton, my great uncle:

'When Alice murdered Betsy Groots
The cunning girl wore Walter's boots
Detective Snooks from Scotland Yard
Measured the footprints, artful card.
When I met Alice six years after
She told me as she shrieked with laughter
   "I murdered Betsy," concealment scorning
"Walter was hanged for it this morning!"'

5

BOARDING SCHOOL certainly made us more appreciative of home, the joy of the holidays amply compensating for all the boredom of the long and seemingly endless terms. Bowhill and Drumlanrig served as hospitals from the outset of the War, which meant that we spent Christmas and Easter at Boughton – where we were entertained by a regiment of Scottish Horse encamped in the park – and August and September at the Lodge, Langholm.

Up till that time only male members of the family had gone to Langholm since it was used exclusively as a shooting lodge, but now that it had to serve as a holiday house we all crammed in. The building consisted of a large dining room and drawing room and many small bedrooms, with an additional 'tin hut' at the back, containing four bedrooms and a bathroom, where younger members of the party were quartered if necessary. Except for the small town of Langholm with its wool and tweed mills, there was nothing but moorland for miles around. Grouse abounded in their thousands, so officers on leave were welcome to come and shoot. Most keepers and estate workers had left to join the Army, so Sybil and I were commandeered to beat and load, each being given a wise old labrador for 'picking up' the birds. Mine was called 'Alice', which seemed rather a mistake! Luckily she made it slightly less confusing by only answering to 'Ulus'. During a day's shooting one walked miles, struggling in and out of peat hags and trudging through heather as high as one's knees. Maybe it was this that made me such an indefatigable walker forever after. There was an unusual number of grouse during those war years. On one occasion, when loading for an elderly 'crack-shot', I marked down the positions of over eighty fallen birds at a single drive on the back of an envelope.

Andrew Smith, the head keeper, was our guide and master, a well respected figure in the neighbourhood and lifelong friend of many of the guests who came to stay over the years. His wife was a wonderful cook and many were the memorable tea-parties we enjoyed in their cottage. There were three fell ponies at Langholm called the 'Black 'un', the 'Grey 'un' and the 'Brune 'un', which were used to carry the hampers of dead game and sometimes to provide a lift for old or infirm guests, who found the walking too tiring. On non-shooting days Andrew Smith, who was a knowledgeable naturalist, used to lead us out riding on these animals. Often such expeditions would last the day, during which we would probably call in on one or other of the tenant farmers scattered around the estate. They and their wives would give us a warm welcome and something good to eat and drink.

One day the 'Black 'un', to receive his carrot, suddenly jumped the railing round his paddock with the ease of a roe deer. 'How splendid!' exclaimed Mary, 'Now we can take him hunting!' And, in the years following the War when the hunt was again in full swing, I would ride him regularly late in the season up in the hill country he knew so well. He loved it as much as I did, never tiring or refusing a jump or stumbling over the 'sheep-drains' which abounded on that difficult ground. He instinctively recognised bogs, stopping to paw the ground and snort so as to let me know to give him his head and find his own way round. Often we would end up the day deep in the moors, twelve or more miles from home, with me quite lost; but I always knew that with a loose rein he would unerringly find the way back without a moment of hesitation. Out of season he lived at Bowhill – pulling the mowing machine or taking household washing to and from Selkirk – a truly remarkable animal, that lived to a good old age of thirty or more.

The Border Esk ran past Langholm, its miles of pools filled with trout and salmon also providing many happy hours of

Seated, aged six, with my sister Mary standing beside me.

In a side-car, aged ten, being driven by my sister Sybil.

My father's caterpillar car, in which he used to tour the estate.

Lions in Kenya. Winner of Diploma of Honour,
Kodak International Salon, World Contest, Geneva 1931.

Supposedly disguised
as a man on the North West
Frontier, 1935.

Going to church at Balmoral as engaged couple
for the first time, 1935: *(left to right)* self,
Prince Henry, Queen Mary (hiding King George).

satisfaction. Night fishing after the sun went down I loved best of all. The fisherman stood silently behind, ready to disentangle my fly if it caught in a tree (or his cap) and to remove it from the jaws of the fish when caught – an operation I could never bear to perform. While we floundered along the river bank between pools he would inform me of the local gossip. I should have preferred silence, with the occasional hoot of an owl, but did not like to tell him so. Some of the fishing was several miles downstream towards the Solway, which necessitated a drive home in the dog-cart pulled by one of the ponies. Clip-clopping along the empty road, moonlight shining through the larch trees on either side, was a perfect end to the day – particularly if a basketful of trout was coming home with us.

Andrew Smith never allowed us an idle moment. 'If it's too wet to shoot it's no' too wet to fish!' he would announce when it rained. For his own private war against the foxes he kept two huge deer hounds. One day the cook at Langholm, Mrs Mac-Donald, left a leg of mutton on the window-sill to cool. 'Algy', one of these pets, got wind of the morsel and made off with it. Later a furious Mrs MacDonald broached the subject with Andrew. 'Dinna fash yersel woman,' he said. 'It'll no' do him a bit of harm.'

Another occupation supervised by Andrew when it was not a shooting day was to take us out on to the hill to pick sphagnum moss as part of the war effort. We would collect it in sacks, and then lay it across the lawn on dust sheets to dry. Afterwards all the bits of heather and peat, dead frogs and other foreign bodies had to be picked out before it could be sent to the hospital. There it was used instead of cottonwool for swabbing out wounds – being full of iodine it was a good disinfectant.

When peace was declared in 1918 I was still at St James's, but left soon after to attend a 'finishing school' at Neuilly on the outskirts of Paris. Here, two charming sisters of the French mistress of St James's ran an establishment for the benefit of eight girls of similar age to myself. We were a happy party and some of us remained friends for many years after. I think I am the only one still alive. We were supposed to improve our French and

[49]

were not allowed to speak English. Cooking and dressmaking were part of our curriculum; the rest of the time we went sight-seeing to art galleries, museums or round Paris itself, occasionally being taken as a special treat to the opera or ballet. I saw Pavlova in *Swan Lake* and was lastingly impressed. The only disagreeable aspect of these outings was the journey on the Metro – the reek of garlic among the pushing crowds I found quite nauseating. After several months of this delightful existence with the Mesdemoiselles Delpierre in the rue Charles Laffitte, I returned to England, supposed ready to burst forth into the world of debutantes and coming-out dances. Apart from having accompanied my mother on one occasion when she took the waters at Aix-les-Bains, this had been my first stay abroad.

By 1916 we had moved into 2 Grosvenor Place. After the war ended my grandfather's tradition of taking a box for the Eton v Harrow cricket match at Lord's was resumed. For the two days of the match enough lunch for 150 guests, many of them ravenous schoolboys, was packed in ice caves and transported daily to the ground. On these occasions the kitchen maids had to be up by about 4 a.m. to hack the ice blocks with pick-axes so that the caves could be bedded in at least one hundredweight of ice chips for the journey. An ice man delivered blocks to the house twice a day. In hot weather ice could be consumed at a rate of ten hundredweight in a week. The first sitting of the Lord's lunch was for Eton boys on their own. When they left they were each tipped a pound by my father.

My father never much enjoyed London life and staying at Grosvenor Place, but he found it quite convenient for visits to the House of Lords and for watching cricket. He seldom went to a club and was apt to sit for hours by a downstairs window at home, playing patience as he worked on the speeches he was always being called upon to deliver. One day, passing on a bus, I overheard two young men in front of me betting each other as to whether or not 'the old bloke' would be in the window playing patience. Sure enough, he was. Sybil, at the early age of eighteen, had married a dashing young cavalry officer and gone off to live in Wiltshire. I missed her and all the fun she brought with her many young friends, who greatly enlivened the rather quiet and melancholy atmosphere of our new London home.

Very shy and rather plump, I made a miserable debut at a dance at Windsor for Princess Mary's birthday, uncomfortably squeezed into a white satin frock. Prince Henry was ill at the time and had to miss the occasion, not that I noticed. I was far too preoccupied with my own anxieties, and spent most of the evening behind a pillar. Attendance at endless deb dances ensued. I thought them dreadful. There was always a chaperone, if not one's mother then one's maid, who had to wait in the cloakroom. The degree to which one had to be chaperoned knew scarcely any bounds. Some cousins, the Lovelaces, lived just around the corner from us in London, but even for their tea parties we had to be dropped and picked up by a maid. The footman would spoil the fun with his dread announcement of her arrival. *Thés dansants* – with cakes, tea and lemonade for refreshment – were popular during the War while rationing still applied. Mothers invariably accompanied their daughters to dances. The girls would be handed a dance-card that they often filled in with a lot of bogus names to make it look as if they were booked up in case someone boring came along searching for a partner. It was difficult to say 'no dances left', because they would insist on asking while looking over one's shoulder. When a little older and more cunning and experienced, we would make daring unchaperoned escapes to a night club. The opportunity for this arose when elderly gentlemen, who seemed to exist solely for this function, gathered up the mothers and took them off to supper or the bridge-room. In this interlude one could be away from the party without much chance of being missed. I never really enjoyed the night club once I got there but was too polite to admit it. I did not drink or smoke and never have done to this day. I danced round and round or sat silently at a table, then insisted I had to go – perhaps rather earlier than necessary – on the pretext that the parents' supper would soon be over. Being presented at Court was somewhat alarming. In my debutante days, one was still required to wear a train and three mysteriously symbolic feathers in one's hair.

When we left school each of us girls was given an annual allowance of £200, paid into our bank accounts in quarterly instalments. We lived at home and an allowance was not expected to cover anything much apart from clothes. Entertainment and travelling costs were never a consideration; tips when one stayed away as a guest were distributed by one's maid, who was then refunded by the house steward. A housemaid could expect to receive a tip of five shillings. Dresses were hideous – very short and straight with a belt around the hips. Sleeves went out of fashion. A young French friend once staying for a Hunt Ball was discovered to have cut off the sleeves of all her evening dresses to accord with the prevailing taste and guiltily hidden them away at the back of a drawer in her dressing table. Her mother must have been horrified.

After a year or two I refused to go to dances unless I knew some of my special friends would be there. My great favourites were the Norfolk family. The Duchess constantly organised vast house-parties to entertain her children, and I spent many happy times at Arundel and Kinharvie, their Scottish home in Dumfriesshire. The major events of the Season – Ascot, Wimbledon, Goodwood – were much as they are today, though Wimbledon then had only two courts. My life, as that of my friends, was principally devoted to pleasure, but in so doing we meant and, I think, did no harm to anybody. Summers in particular were a succession of country house parties, with life in London filling the gaps. The street outside Grosvenor Place was sharply uphill and was always a struggle for the dray horses as they heaved past in the dawn bound for the markets at Covent Garden with the new day's vegetables. I would lie awake, perhaps only just returned from a dance, feeling sorry for them as I listened to the shouts of the carters and the merciless crack of their whips.

6

FOR ME the early Twenties was a relaxed and carefree time. At Bowhill during the winter months hunting provided my main occupation and source of exhilaration. I possessed only one horse of my own, but fortunately my brothers were kind enough to lend me theirs should they have one spare. For two seasons I was lent a lovely thoroughbred by a friend who had to go abroad with his regiment; so what with the addition of an occasional mount on one of the hunt horses I did not do too badly and managed two if not three hunts a week. I thought of little else, which seems strange to me now but gives me sympathy for those many young people who partake more than ever before in this particular sport. There is, I have found, much one can learn from it that is helpful in every day life: endurance, quickness and perception, speed of decision, 'give and take', infinite patience and tolerance from handling horses, not to mention a 'bump of locality' and sense of direction that was to be particularly helpful to me at a later date in East Africa.

The Buccleuch Hunt covered an extensive area and its follow-ers were apt to come out only when the 'meet' happened to be within reach of where they lived; so there were never the large crowds that often spoil the fun of hunting in the popular midland counties. I knew everyone by sight and name and a friendly crowd they were; most of them belonging to families who had farmed, lived and hunted there for generations.

In those days when 'army leave' was fairly easily obtained,

Billy would frequently arrive home for sporting weekends accompanied by brother officers; and quite often amongst them would be my future husband. Contact with Prince Henry was not confined to these hunting and shooting parties at Bowhill or Drumlanrig, because when the regiment was stationed within reach of London he was also a frequent visitor to Grosvenor Place. He was expected to stay at Buckingham Palace if he was passing a night in London, but this necessitated his saying exactly where he was going and what he was doing; so his use of our house was kept a secret, even from my parents. In fact only Rowland would know the exact arrangements. Billy and Prince Henry used to arrive late in the evening, change, go out to their party, return for a few hours sleep and leave by seven to be on parade by eight. The family were usually in bed before and after they had come and gone.

Cavalry officers from the regiment stationed in Edinburgh would keep their horses at the stables in St Boswells and come and hunt at the weekends, often staying with us at Bowhill. Amongst these were Major and Mrs Tiarks. Had he lived how proud the Major, later the Colonel, would have been of his grandson Mark Phillips. Others included Charles and Elspeth Miller, destined to join us during our stay in Australia as Private Secretary and Lady-in-Waiting. Many, alas, failed to return from the War, notably Ranulph Twistleton-Wykeham-Fiennes, grandfather of the explorer. A younger hunt follower, whose future one could hardly have foretold, was a small plump boy on an even plumper pony led on a rein by a large Mama on a vast horse. This was Willie Whitelaw. His father had been killed in the First World War and his widowed mother came to live in the Borders. His grandfather, who lived in Edinburgh, was one of my father's greatest friends.

Another enthusiastic member of the hunt was Earl Haig, the Field Marshal. I often found myself riding with him alongside on the way back to the kennels where my horse was kept. His home at Bemersyde was a few miles farther, on the same road. He was a delightful and friendly person and his daughters were our closest friends. When frost made the ground too hard for hunting we

[54]

and the young Haigs would organise paper-chases through the woods or mixed ice hockey matches. Once we even played the 13/18 Hussars at their barracks just outside Edinburgh. The matches were always furious and fast and on this occasion Doria Haig broke a bone in her ankle. On our return home Lord Haig was most annoyed and asked why on earth the referee had let things get so out of hand. We then had to admit that there had not been a referee. This made him even more angry, but in the end all was forgiven.

After Doria Haig's wedding to my cousin Andrew Scott, we had a picnic on the road home, by the Grey Mare's Tail waterfall in Dumfriesshire. It was a famous beauty spot, and afterwards when we came screaming down the hill dressed in our wedding finery, the men all in top hats and tail coats, a party of sightseers gave one look and rushed in terror for the safety of their charabanc.

Like myself, Xandra, another of the Haig daughters, helped with the Girl Guides and one summer her troop from Roxburghshire joined with mine from Selkirk at the same camp. Most inconsiderately she brought her father's camp-bed, a very grand iron affair weighing a ton. It would not fit into any tent so the end had to stick out into the field. It was the only bed we had and could not have been more of a nuisance. The camp itself, however, was a great success. The Guides all cried the first night because they were homesick and again on the last night because they did not want to go back!

By the time I was grown-up cars were fairly commonplace. Most of them were open, with hoods that went up when needed. When we grew older my sisters and I were given a Morris Cowley to share between us. Cars had balloon tyres at that date – if anything pricked them they burst – and one day as the three of us were merrily spinning along to Edinburgh that is exactly what happened. I found myself standing in a field of turnips. Mary emerged out of the ditch at the other side of the road, but where was Angela? After much agitated searching we discovered her underneath a bramble bush. She proved to be the only one of us that was hurt – her collar-bone was broken. After a lift home in a kindly passing car we left her in hospital with everything duly taken care of. Mary and I took the plunge and broke the news to my father. He was wrestling with *The Times* crossword, and did not look up while we nervously awaited his reaction. There was a long silence. 'What's a three letter word for sheep?' he asked. 'Ewe?' we suggested. And that was that.

One of my father's greatest sources of pleasure was his caterpillar car. This was a sort of small tank, open and with caterpillar tracks instead of wheels. There was virtually nowhere it could not go and we travelled in it a lot together around the woods and farms. He liked nothing better than to frighten the wits out of unsuspecting guests by taking them for drives up and down the most precipitous banks on the estate. He got the idea of having one of these machines from the Duke of Beaufort, who used one for following the hounds.

We were easily and innocently amused by today's standards: acting and paper games, the various forms of hide n' seek, and more energetic favourites liked billiard fives and 'Freda', which entailed tearing round the table at great speed. Practical jokes were also considered extremely funny. These took numerous forms, from simple apple-pie beds to more complicated tortures, usually reserved for pompous young men. We would stitch mustard plasters in the seat of their evening trousers and watch them suffer agonies at dinner. It was this sort of behaviour that made Prince Henry so much appreciate life with the Scotts. He was treated just like everyone else. My mother insisted on rolling out a red carpet for him when he arrived, but the rest of us ridiculed this and I think he found it an embarrassment. No fuss was made of him otherwise, and to me at first he was significant only as one of the more regular visitors from among my brother Billy's regimental friends – shy, unassuming and always happy to join in the fun.

In April 1924 I had my first glimpse of Africa. Sybil had had a bad attack of influenza and her doctors advised her to take a recuperative holiday in the sun, so she decided she would like to visit North Africa. She was married by then but nothing would induce her husband to accompany her – he was busy with their

[56]

farm in Wiltshire and anyway hated going abroad – so it was planned that I and a mutual friend of ours, Nellie Baillie-Hamilton, would come along instead. Finally, an admirer of Sybil's – a staid and very proper gentleman called Colonel Southey – said he would like to come too, and as he had a large car we all decided this would be a good idea. The party was completed by a rather ancient lady's maid, who also acted as Nellie's chaperone. With the Colonel at the wheel we set off to tour Algeria. It proved a happy tour with beautiful scenery and warm sun, and certainly did the trick as far as Sybil's health was concerned. Nellie was a great character, whose spirits and good humour never flagged. She ragged poor Colonel Southey mercilessly, upsetting him by pretending to have fallen madly in love with some undesirable sheik, from whose clutches it seemed that the Colonel would imminently have to rescue her. He bore it all very well. For me a memorable moment in the adventure took place at the oasis town of Biskra. Here there was an old seer who told our fortunes by making marks in the sand. When it came to my turn he took a long while and then said in French that I would marry someone of higher station than myself. Since I was a Duke's daughter this seemed rather unlikely to me. But he insisted. 'I see a crown and much to do with the Army. You will travel greatly, many long distances.' I thought this all sounded nonsense.

Mr Rowland was now established as Head Steward of the Buccleuch household. According to his written account, every day at 7.30 a.m. he would go through the house we happened to be in at the time, seeing that all was in order. Then, after his breakfast at 8.30, he checked all the clocks to see that they were telling the correct time and settled down to his routine cellar or office work. Running the household was still a massive enterprise. Untold tons of logs and three to four hundred tons of coke and coal were alone used every year in fuelling it. Christmas at Bowhill continued to be as much of a feast as at Dalkeith. The festivities lasted a month, with an average of eighty mouths to be fed at every meal. One year no fewer than 220 people were given Christmas dinner. The standard order was for 150 lbs of turkey.

The business of moving to one house from another was miraculously completed in a matter of two days. This included the transport of 250 pieces of luggage, collectively weighing no less than eight tons.

Delivering food from the kitchens to the dining room along the endless passages at Drumlanrig required split-second timing if soufflés were not to fall flat or the weekly haunch of roasted venison arrive stone cold. Once an oddman took a wrong turning and got lost in the house with the second course for dinner. Even guests could go astray, especially after the port and cigars. To prevent this there was a red line painted along the passage wall to indicate the route between the smoking or billiard room, in a remote wing of the Castle, and the main building. It was considered bad form to smoke when the ladies of the house might be around, so the gentlemen were given this special room well out of smelling distance.

The cellars at Bowhill and Drumlanrig each contained two 54-gallon barrels of whisky – the equivalent of 100 dozen bottles – which were never allowed to be more than half empty; and there were similar supplies of sherry and port. All of this and much more was the responsibility of the steward. It is easy to see why the stock response to every problem was: 'I'll ask Mr Rowland.'

This watchword was used to ultimate effect one morning when my father asked a footman if it was raining. 'I'll ask Mr Rowland, Your Grace,' came the reply. My father summoned Rowland. 'Has that footman any brains at all?' he said. 'If he had any more he would not be here,' answered Rowland. My father frequently closeted himself with Rowland after dinner, to discuss family matters and current events quite as much as the problems of the household. Sometimes they talked till the early hours of the morning, my father pacing up and down as if he was back on the deck of a ship. Rowland was no less a confidante of ours. It was not done to have drinks before dinner in the way that it is now, at least my father would not allow it, so Rowland used to supply my brothers and their friends with a tipple in the steward's room at 6.30. Only my mother noticed. 'Why, I

[58]

wonder does Billy always have to see Rowland every evening?' she puzzled. But, of course, his secret was secure.

In 1926 I went again to Africa but this time to the Cape. The Earl of Athlone was Governor-General of South Africa at the time and my elder sister Mida was lady-in-waiting to Princess Alice. When she got engaged to Commander Geoffrey Hawkins, ADC to the Governor-General, it was decided that it was more convenient to hold the wedding out there. My mother and I were invited to stay at Government House. The ceremony took place at the newly built Cathedral, Cape Town. My mother's brother Colonel Harry Bridgeman came down from his farm in the Transvaal to give my sister away. I accepted with delight an invitation to stay on for awhile, which enabled me to see more of South Africa under very enjoyable circumstances.

South Africa in those days offered no hint of future disharmony. It seemed the most blissfully happy place. One never saw a glum face. The Athlones were more than kind and took me around with them on various tours and as a result I got quite a broad picture in the relatively short time I was there, as well as the chance to develop a very sincere devotion to my host and hostess. Perhaps the most memorable expedition in which I took part was a shooting safari in Zululand. This took place during an Easter holiday for the staff. The party consisted of the two ADCs, Mida, my brother-in-law and myself. We took no tents, and our entire equipment was put on a wagon and drawn by twelve donkeys. One morning at crack of dawn the others all went off to shoot rhino. Princess Alice had allowed me to go only on condition that I did not take part in the shooting of this particularly dangerous animal, so honouring my promise to her I stayed and tidied up at camp with the Africans. Suddenly there was not a soul to be seen, the Africans were all huddled under the wagon. Glancing round I saw mother rhino and her baby trotting down towards us. I hid under one of the camp-beds, praying she would not scent me, and to my great relief she passed by. The hunters later returned, exhausted and empty-handed, having not seen a rhino all day. Afterwards I wished I had been bolder and taken a photograph.

On another occasion Sir Richard and Lady Howard Vyse – Sir Richard nicknamed 'Wombat' because of his resemblance to that animal – arrived at Government House in the course of their honeymoon. Unwisely they mentioned that their next stop was Victoria Falls. 'Oh, Alice hasn't seen Victoria Falls,' said Princess Alice forcefully. 'You'd better take her along with you!' The last thing they can have wanted was company, but they obligingly agreed and off I went, with Mida's enormously fat maid to look after me. Needless to say they could not have been more welcoming and indeed protective. When they went to see me safely on to the sleeper for Natal to visit my Uncle Harry Bridgeman, Hermione Vyse was put out to find that my maid had been consigned to a different part of the train. 'Who's next door to Lady Alice Scott?' she demanded. It turned out to be Ivor Guest, later Lord Wimborne, a young man whom I knew vaguely from England. Hermione confronted him immediately. 'You can't possibly be next to Alice Scott,' she explained briskly. 'You must move into another carriage. Her maid has got to go in here.' The disgruntled young man was put to flight. We subsequently met on many occasions and I am glad to say he bore me no malice.

South Africa was idyllic, but its legacy turned out to be a frightening bout of cerebral malaria. One morning I woke up with a mosquito bite on my elbow. Apparently the train I was on had stopped overnight in a cerebral malarial district, but not knowing this at the time I thought no more of it till, crossing the Equator on the homeward voyage, I developed a fever and soon fell unconscious. It was a horrid experience. In delirium I thought I was a tree in a tin. All my limbs were growing and I could not get them out, so that the more they grew the more they ached. Luckily the greatest living authority on tropical diseases, Dr Rabagliate, happened to be on board, and one of the passengers had some dope that pulled me through, but I was lucky not to die.

I convalesced at Boughton. Nothing could have been more of a tonic. After dinner, we and our guests would go out into the woods to hear the singing of the nightingales. It usually ended – at least for the younger members of the house party – with a rough and tumble in the bushes. Another pastime I especially associate with Boughton, though we played it as fervently at other house parties, is treasure hunting. This involved going off in pairs after dinner – a boy and a girl – with a list of about twenty items that had to be collected as soon as possible from the surrounding countryside. Whoever arrived home first with their full consignment were declared the winners. Inevitably there were silly things to be fetched, like Mrs. Corrigan's stays, or ones that involved dare-devil 'burglaries' on neighbouring country houses, perhaps obliging the hunters to motor twenty miles or more. It was great fun for us, but must at times have been very irritating for other people. It was a great age for after-dinner games and we would often settle down to charades, or some sort of paper game like Consequences. At the time, I remember, some of the responses people invented seemed very daring, but I am afraid the young today would think them boringly innocent.

Our most intriguing neighbour was probably Mr Brudenell of Deene, who wore a square top hat and long cloth cloak even indoors to keep out the draught. I first met him when I was about fourteen. My mother had announced: 'We must have the new owner of Deene Park over for lunch. I believe he's stone-deaf so we'll have to shout.' On the appointed day my mother duly shouted at Mr Brudenell through half the meal and then, turning to Mida, said 'Your turn now.' Mida took over the shouting and after lunch we all shouted 'goodbye' to him. A few weeks later at a flower show I was again introduced to Mr Brudenell. 'Ah yes,' he said, 'you and your sisters made rude remarks about me all through lunch. I can lip read you know!'

Another time at Boughton my father had a professor of forestry over from Cambridge for lunch. Afterwards they toured the woods with the retired head forester, Mr Neill. When the tour was over my father turned to Mr Neill and said: 'Well, have you learnt anything from the Professor?' 'Not a damn bit! It was all a lot of rot!' The embarrassed professor then left. 'Neill,' said my father, 'you should not have said that to the Professor . . . but I agree with you.'

A delightful friend of both my father and mother was Lady

Mabel Howard. She often came to stay and regaled us with amusing stories. She drove herself, most dangerously and usually on the wrong side of the road, in an aged Morris Oxford. The car was named 'The Humble One' and was well-known wherever she went – most people stopping and going as far off the road as possible when they saw it coming. My sister and I quite often stayed with her at Greystoke Castle. We always enjoyed it there, in spite of it being haunted and creepy at night, with no electric light and badly fitting windows and doors creaking and banging. She lived on her own but asked endless guests of all ages, who were welcome at any time. She would always arrange amusing expeditions for us and it was never less than the greatest fun to be with her. We all loved her dearly – as did many in the county of Cumberland and the town of Carlisle, where she did endless good work for the benefit of the needy.

Her sister Lady Nina Balfour, another particular favourite of my father's, was one of our neighbours, presiding at Newton Don in the Borders. She was also a great character and an incorrigible match-maker, which was rather off-putting, but there was no hostess in Scotland who could equal the deliciousness of her food, her impeccable taste and flair for a party. She also had a rollicking sense of humour. One of her favourite jokes against herself concerned one of the many balls at Newton Don, and an elderly waiter who had been engaged to do the formal announcement of the guests. He was not very experienced at the job and shortly after the start of the presentations he was flummoxed by the arrival of two horse-drawn buses from which large numbers of people descended. He correctly gauged that this was the Duke of Roxburghe and his party, but despairing of their numbers, proceeded to announce them collectively as 'The Party from Floors'. Then, met by a wave of arrivals from the second bus, he bellowed: 'And some mair of 'em!'

Aunt Celia, Countess of Scarborough, was another of my father's favourites. She was not always popular, because she would insist on attending the grouse shoots carrying a yellow umbrella. If it started to rain in the middle of a drive – as it usually seemed to – up went the umbrella and all the grouse flew into the next county. I think my father rather encouraged her because it made all his relations, who took shooting a great deal more seriously than he did, beside themselves with rage. My mother was not interested in the shooting, but she was subtle in showing her disapproval. She just pretended she could not tell the difference between one bird and another. It was a fiction she kept up till the end of her life. My brother William and his wife Rachel were once staying at Branxholm, the home of her old age, and Rachel remembers her saying to the cook: 'Lord William will have a cold wing of snipe for breakfast.' A snipe is, of course, about the size of a sparrow.

An aunt who made a great impression on me was my mother's younger sister, Helena, Lady Sefton. The other Bridgeman aunts and my mother tended to be rather prim, but Aunt Nellie could not have been more forthright or spirited. Long before the First War she shocked her relations by wearing trousers and going off big-game shooting with a boyfriend – needless to say, it was the trousers that caused the worst scandal. In the last War she drove lorries, though by then she was well over seventy. She was terrifically given to good works and a very religious person. I was very impressed when she once took me down to the canteen in the docks where she often helped cook breakfast for the merchant seamen who had come in the night before or at break of dawn.

Possessed as I was by a strong sense that I ought to be doing something to help others, I went one night a week to help the Captain of the Selkirk Guides and Rangers, and also joined the Selkirk branch of the Red Cross, eventually becoming a V.A.D. My mother disapproved of this, thinking it wrong and dangerous that I should drive myself to and from Selkirk – four miles distant – alone and after dark through the winter months. She would probably have been even more disapproving if she had known that on the way home I invariably gave a lift to old Tom the oddman, who regularly walked to the town in all weathers for a drink at the pub. For the Red Cross Camp one year I ventured on my own as far as Dunecht in Aberdeenshire. The Camp was for the whole of Scotland, and I got to know many extremely nice people whom I was later to come across again in the War at First Aid Posts, Hospital Supply Depots or engaged in various other useful capacities. Taking on a particularly hazardous stretch of road known as 'Devil's Elbow' in a Morris Oxford was an alarming experience, the engine boiling like a kettle before I was half-way up the mountain.

Ski-ing at St Moritz in January of 1927 and 1929 provides some of my happiest memories. How very different St Moritz was in those days to the crowded resort it has become. The few people who did go were mostly English and American. I went out with the Haddingtons, Xandra Haig and Sarah Haddington's sister Dorothy. Being Canadian Sarah and Dorothy were both expert skiers and skaters. We joined many friends and acquaintances at the Suvretta Hotel, at that time run by an Englishman, Colonel Bond, who appeared to be a tremendous friend of everybody. It was like staying in a private house-party. Those one did not know already one soon became friendly with, through meeting over a 'sun downer' or joining up for dinner together.

There were no ski-lifts and it was quite an effort struggling up the slopes to the start of the runs. Luckily, as a result of much riding, I was very fit and had the necessary muscles for controlling my skis. It did not take me long to get going easily without too many tumbles. Sometimes amongst the breathless climbers one would find Lady Astor, with her sister Mrs Brand alongside. They were expert skiers and enjoyed the fun as much as anyone, in spite of being elderly compared to most of us. Nancy Astor, through her fame and force of character, tended to preside over the party. She was a lot of fun but could sometimes be rather cruel and sarcastic, as when she deliberately embarrassed people in public. During a lull at dinner, for instance, she might suddenly fasten on some shy young girl and shout across the table: 'Who is that young man I saw you having chocolate with?' The victim, not surprisingly, was apt to be mortified by the unexpected attention which was focused on her.

Occasionally we would go ski-ing by moonlight. This entailed riding in a snow-cat – a vehicle with caterpillar wheels – which took us to the start of a long run down a wide track through the forest. It was most romantic, with the full moon casting blue shadows from the snow-covered fir trees on either side. At the end of the run we assembled for hot soup at a small chalet and from there drove back to the hotel. Sometimes we would go to Silsmaria, a small resort on the border with Italy. For this we hired a horse-drawn sleigh with three or four of us sitting inside and two following on skis holding on to a rope. With tinkling bells attached to the horses and beautiful scenery all around us, this was a charming experience. We had friends practising for the Cresta Run and sometimes went to watch them. Xandra and I persuaded them to arrange for us to go down the last lap one Sunday morning when the Run was closed to competitions. I am sure this must have been most irresponsible on their part, however, as it snowed heavily the night before, the jaunt was not possible. Just as well, no doubt.

There were spectacular skating competitions on the Lake and most nights a party of some sort. One particularly memorable one was given by Mary Ashley to announce her engagement to Bobbie Cunningham Reid. There must have been thirty or more of us seated around a large round table and a very hilarious party it was. On another evening there was a fancy dress ball. I went as Jackie Coogan – and by borrowing the right sort of cap I made a passable impression. They were very happy days and over all too soon – three weeks seeming to be the prescribed length of a visit.

1929 represented something of a watershed in my life. Apart from anything else it was the year my father first showed symptoms of the cancer – undiagnosed at the time – from which he was eventually to die. It was not an easy period. My mother was devoted to my father and terribly worried about his health, but her anxiety and fuss irritated him. Things were not improved by the arrival of a permanent nurse in the form of Miss Dickie. He enjoyed her company, and showed his gratitude by giving her a pearl necklace and fur coat. Not unnaturally this made my mother jealous. I think she was also slightly jealous of me, because I too at that time was favoured by my father. As a result I felt uneasy at home and restless in other ways. The unfulfilled promise I had made in return for my life nagged at my conscience. Boyfriends were getting over-friendly and increasingly I did not know how to cope. I began to realise that the people I met were 'birds of a feather' – young men, in particular that is, who seemed to think of nothing but hunting, shooting, fishing and point-to-points. I wanted to find a different kind of life and to meet other types of people.

It was at this time that my Uncle Francis Scott, his wife and two lovely little girls arrived at Drumlanrig on holiday from their farm in Kenya. They suggested I come and stay with them for an extended visit, and assured me that there were plenty of things I could do to make myself useful. Coming at a moment of such uncertainty the offer could not have been more tempting, but nevertheless I found it hard to accept. There was my hunting to give up, and the sadness of leaving my father. Uncle Francis and his family left. I remained in doubt. Then one day when I was out for a walk, turning the question over in my mind for the umpteenth time, a roe deer suddenly started up. It leapt a fence and galloped away towards the hills. 'There,' I thought. 'That's an omen. I must get up and gallop away too.' And with no further ado I went home and wrote a letter of acceptance.

7

It was with some concern and sadness that I made this great decision to move so far away, leaving my father in none too good a state of health. I knew he appreciated my company and was amused by my flow of local gossip and any funny stories I could collect, not to mention my help with the crossword puzzles. He may have wondered why I should want to leave such a comfortable existence to visit a country so unknown and lacking in comforts. Maybe too he envied me, going off to a life so free of regulations and social responsibilities. He was very fond of his youngest brother and concerned about his severely wounded leg; and perhaps guessed that I could be of much help to him and his wife and family. Whatever his feelings, my father generously gave me my ticket for the journey and money for a car and petrol – and, much to my relief, I later discovered he had also cleared my large overdraft at the bank!

My Uncle and Aunt for their part suggested I bring a girlfriend with me, and a lovely and delightful friend of mine, Marye Pole Carew, agreed to come along. So, in the autumn of 1929, we set out on our great adventure, by train to Genoa and then by ship to Mombasa. The SS *Llandaff Castle* in which we travelled took some weeks to reach Kenya, stopping at Port Said and Aden en route. Having travelled to and from the Cape by the West Coast of Africa in the *Windsor Castle* and *Kildonan Castle* it made a change to see something of the East Coast. Amongst the passengers were a few known to my Uncle and Aunt – settlers and officials returning to Kenya and Uganda. Lady Delamere who was among them owned a large property in Kenya. She was an attractive and amusing person and exceptionally good company. I was to meet her and her family on numerous occasions in the years to come.

It was a night's journey from Mombasa to Nairobi, and none too comfortable a night with jolts and jerks and ringing of bells when the train came to a halt at various small stations along the line. It was with relief that we found ourselves at Government House, at last able to remove the coating of red dust from our faces and clothes. The Governor, Sir Edward Grigg (later Lord Altrincham) and his good-looking wife Joan, gave us a warm welcome. Government House, designed by Sir Herbert Baker – an architect well known for many houses in South Africa as well as other Government Houses – is a most attractive building surrounded by a large and lovely garden. Here we stayed in great comfort for a few days before setting off to my Uncle's farm of Deloraine.

The so-called 'main road' from Nairobi to Eldoret and eventually Uganda was exceedingly rough, with innumerable potholes and ruts, patches of corrugation and clouds of red dust most of the way. It was a slow journey – the 140 miles took us most of a day – but for Marye and me, our eyes glued to the bush and plains, it could hardly have been more exciting. We saw countless wild animals: giraffe, ostrich, wildebeest, zebra and antelope were everywhere, often scarcely bothering to remove themselves from the road, while nervous families of monkeys or a leopard would occasionally dash across in front of us. Today the number of animals has drastically diminished, the road one speeds along at seventy mph is tarmac. The pioneering sense of those times has long gone too, but the story is not lost. The days of the settlers who went to make a life in Kenya in the early decades of the present century are delightfully recalled in *They made it their Home* – a collection of stories with an introduction by Elspeth Huxley, published in 1962. Of all the books I have read, this best covers the period before and while I was there.

Hot and tired and once more covered in dust we eventually

arrived at our destination. Here I was to make my home for over a year. A dozen or more Africans were assembled to greet us. Hearty handshakes and chatter were exchanged by all and much interest shown in Marye and me – new arrivals were a rarity. There too were Uncle Francis, Aunt Eileen, my cousins Pam and Moy and the governess.

In 1920 my uncle, along with a number of other ex-army officers, decided to start a new life farming in Kenya. After the War the British Government had decided to encourage British citizens to settle in the colony and they organised a lottery in England to this end apportioning land to all who entered for it. My uncle's number when drawn turned out to be a piece of land very distant from town or railway. As his daughters were then aged only four and two, this property seemed too isolated for him to risk taking it on. Luckily, however, someone proved willing to make an exchange, so he ended up with a place halfway between Nairobi and Eldoret. In terms of communications this was ideal, being near to where a hospital was to be built twenty-eight miles away in Nakuru and only four miles from the nearest railway station at Rongai.

When my uncle and aunt arrived with their two small children and the indomitable Miss Loder, my aunt's maid, they had to live in three mud huts while they organised the building of the house – later to be named 'Deloraine' after a hill on the family estate in Selkirkshire. Bricks were made locally by Indians, who were the only local people capable of that sort of work. Deloraine was one of the few houses in the colony to have a second storey. By the time I arrived there was already a lovely garden of well-kept lawns and shrubs.

Miss Loder had established herself as something of a local legend. She was everything: housekeeper, nanny, cook, dairy maid. My aunt left her in complete control and accordingly she would be on the go all day – cursing, screaming, shouting and generally bullying the African 'boys', who took it all with the greatest good humour. There were many house-boys – completely uneducated and speaking only Swahili. They could not have been more good-humoured or obliging. The same applied to the workers on the farm. In most cases the men were incorrigibly lazy. They would sit gossiping, dash out and work madly at the sound of someone coming, then stop the moment they could get away with it again. This was the tradition: the women worked, the men did not – to do so, for them, was an indignity. The attitude was general but its effects were particularly noticeable at Deloraine because of the spirit of toleration that presided there. Francis Scott was one of those people who never thought ill of anyone. As a result a succession of somewhat unhelpful managers was left in charge, while he attended to his Parliamentary duties in Nairobi as a member of the Legislative Council.

Aunt Eileen was a most unsuitable person to embark on life in such primitive conditions; nevertheless she did so with the greatest courage and good humour. As a girl she had lived all her life in the height of comfort, first at her home at Minto in Scotland and later as a daughter of the Viceroy of India; she tried to lead a life in Kenya as near as possible to what she had become accustomed to in the past. Deloraine was grandly furnished with family pictures, and silver was laid for every meal. She would rise late in the mornings and always take great care of her appearance, never appearing without a hat and gloves and usually with a parasol as well. The Africans found it all most intriguing. However, she did design and start the lovely gardens, which now have flowering shrubs of brilliant colours nine or ten feet tall; and she also made a kitchen-garden on either side of a small stream, in which were grown many English vegetables, including asparagus. Fig trees did well but the figs had to be enclosed in little bags, otherwise they would be eaten by monkeys. Apart from this she read novels and, whenever it was possible, played bridge. She loved music and the theatre and must have missed these sadly while in Kenya. Gramophone records were the only music to be heard – apart from native tom toms beating in the distant villages.

Mida, when visiting Deloraine in the early days, was invited to a dance some forty miles away and a young man offered to drive her there. On hearing this Aunt Eileen felt bound to accompany her as chaperone. A deck chair was erected in the back of the box-body car, and with Aunt Eileen perched there, they set off. Mida and the young man chatted away and arrived at the party in no time, only to discover to their horror that Aunt Eileen had vanished. Everyone was in a state of confused indecision when, to their profound relief, she re-appeared in someone else's car. Her rescuers had been travelling through the bush when, to their amazement, they had found their way blocked by a lady sitting in a deck chair under an elegant parasol. It was typical that when I first arrived in Africa she insisted on only two things: that I should wear a red flannel spine pad and a red lining to my hat. Everyone wore a wide-brimmed felt hat in those days, as protection from what were generally considered to be the lethal rays of the sun. Both spine-pad and hat proved tiresome in a hot country. I wore them religiously till I arrived on my second trip to find, to my relief, that such garments were no longer thought to be necessary.

Of course not all the African men were lazy, and Uncle Francis was especially blessed in that he had a Masai tribesman of extraordinary devotion as his personal servant. This was unusual because the Masai were the proudest of tribes and normally deemed any kind of service beneath contempt; but Ehru, my uncle's servant, was exceptional in that a white man had saved his life. During the First War he had been a soldier in the Kenya African rifles and, after a skirmish with the Germans, had been wounded and left to die on the battlefield. One of the settlers, Mervyn Ridley, his officer at the time, bravely rescued him and subsequently saw to it that he was nursed back to health. Ehru, in return, pledged his life to him. Mervyn Ridley was in no need of further employees at that point, so he passed Ehru on to my uncle. He proved the most faithful servant anyone could want and was dearly loved by all.

I was scarcely less privileged in my own servant, Kimani. He was in his mid-twenties and acted as my maid, motor boy, bodyguard, in fact everything. Kimani was assigned to me as soon as I arrived. I paid him sixpence a day, which covered his food and all living expenses, and I bought him his clothes – several pairs of shorts, some loose, white, shirt-like garments and a red tarboosh and blankets. If needed, I would also buy some extras for him, like wood. We motored hundreds of miles alone together with no trace of anxiety on my part. No one could have been a more dependable or trustworthy companion. If we stayed somewhere and he suspected another boy of mischief, he would ask me to hand over my money, jewellery and anything else I had that might tempt a thief and would take it into his own safe-keeping for the night. To have such confidence nowadays would be rare.

Once Kimani came to me and asked if he could have the day off the next day. I agreed but asked him the reason. 'I have to cook something that I must take to a particular old tree because my little son is ill and the witch-doctor says I must do that to make him well again.' 'But Kimani,' I remonstrated, 'I thought you were a Christian?' 'Oh yes I am,' he said seriously, 'but it's just as well to be on the safe side.' This conversation was, of course, conducted in Swahili, few Africans at that time being able to speak English.

On one occasion his zeal for my well-being was overdone. Finding some brand-new laces in my shoes instead of the old worn-out and knotted ones, I asked him where he had got them. With great pride he said he had taken them out of one of the other Bwana's shoes.

'But that's awful, Kimani,' I said in horror. 'It's stealing!'

'Oh no,' he replied confidently. 'Kimani not stealing for Kimani, it is for Memsahib.'

'But that's worse,' I said, 'because it makes me a thief.'

'Oh no,' said Kimani. 'Memsahib did not do it.'

There was nothing more to be said. That was how he had worked it all out and his way of thinking!

Necessity soon forced me to pick up enough of the language to make myself understood. Every white person was given a name by the Africans. My aunt, for instance, always wore ear-rings so she was called Memsahib 'Kingeli', which means 'ear-rings'. When I arrived for the first time I was named Memsahib 'Mhowa', which means 'flower', because I liked to pick bunches of wild flowers for my room. Giggling hordes of children from

[72]

the village would invariably follow me around on my walks, mimicking my movements with glee and picking vast bunches themselves which they would subsequently press on me. They just thought I was rather dotty to do such a thing, but the local witch-doctor was positively disapproving. If I passed his house on my way home he would give me a nasty look which I returned with my sweetest smile, annoying him even more. My 'Memsahib Mhowa' days, however, were relatively short-lived, because when it was learned that I had flown away and returned again by air I was re-christened Memsahib 'Ndegi' meaning 'bird'. There were only a few private planes in Kenya at the time – and people who travelled in them were viewed in consequence with understandable awe by the locals.

Kenya seemed so peaceful in those days. The Africans one met were always smiling and contented; there were spectacular amounts of game of every species and the bush, as one drove along, was a glory of magnificent cedars, podocarpus and crimson flame trees. In other ways, however, travelling was not always a joy. The roads, even the main roads out of Nairobi, were formed only of packed mud, which soon deteriorated into wheel tracks, often rutted so deeply that you had to move to one side or the other and make a fresh track. Much of the soil, known as 'black cotton', became impassable and like a peat bog after rain.

Box-body cars – mine was a Citroen – were the most commonly used at that time, and one had to put chains on the tyres when it was wet. A roll of chicken-wire was also carried to lay on the mud or for crossing a sandy river bed if the chains could still not get a grip. Bridges were a rarity, and when there at all often consisted of no more than a couple of stout planks to which the wheels yet again had to be precariously aligned. Often fords or dry river-beds were suddenly turned into torrents by the after effects of electric storms taking place in a different part of the country upstream from where one was. At these times the motor boy, who was always in attendance, would survey the prospects and if necessary lead the car through the flood, water to his knees. If it proved too deep there was nothing to be done but wait till the level dropped. As a result bedding and food were usually carried. The chances of meeting other travellers were remote.

Having omitted to have her injection before leaving England, Marye fell ill shortly after our arrival with a mild attack of typhoid fever necessitating her removal into Nakuru War Memorial hospital. Visiting her was made no easier by the fact that it was the rainy season. One morning, therefore, when the day broke fine and sunny I took the opportunity of paying her a call. I started for home under a bright sky with plenty of time to spare before nightfall. However, as was always likely to happen, the day turned cloudy and threatening and soon we were engulfed in a downpour. Driving became very difficult and we went slower and slower. Eventually we arrived at a fork in the road and stopped, because I could not remember which to follow. Not having learned any Swahili at that point I was unable to consult Kimani, so there was no alternative but to plunge on into what seemed to me to be ever more unfamiliar country. My growing despair was then lifted by the encouraging sight of the tail-lights of a car ahead, and soon I was behind it, hooting for all I was worth to make it stop. The driver appeared not to hear, and for all my miles of hooting did not stop till we arrived at his front door. When he emerged he looked at me with astonishment.

'I've been hooting and hooting, hoping you would stop and show us back to the right road,' I said with exasperation.

'I'm so sorry,' he replied, 'but you see I've been expecting a friend to come and stay. I thought it was him hooting just to let me know he was there.'

'Well, it wasn't,' I said rather tetchily, and I explained our predicament while he asked me in for a cup of tea.

'So,' he said eventually, giving me a kindly smile. 'You'd better stay the night.'

'I can't do that,' I said, 'because my uncle and aunt would be so worried and upset.'

As soon as he discovered who they were he become most respectful and insisted on escorting me for several miles and seeing me safely across the river close to our farm. I never met him again, but my uncle and aunt knew of him and much later I heard he had been killed while on safari.

Marye soon recovered enough to leave hospital and we took her for Christmas to Mervyn Ridley's house, Kapsiliat, up north beyond Eldoret, and then back to Government House for the New Year. There was a large party there for polo, racing and other festivities, and among the guests was Sir William Gowers, Governor of Uganda, nicknamed 'Wicked Willie' because of his roving eye for the ladies. He thought Marye and me were rather fun, and promised that if we were to come to Uganda he would personally escort us to the Mountains of the Moon. We accepted this with much joy but unfortunately, by the time we arrived at Entebbe, Sir William was indisposed with phlebitis. However, he was as true to his word as he could be, and lent us his ADC, Sidney de Salis, to escort us. To complete the party we collected John McNab whom we had met on board our ship on the way out. Before we left Deloraine Aunt Eileen had told us to take matches and a candle with us; this we did, and it was just as well as we found no lights at all in the bungalow at the Crater Lake. There were alarming grunting noises all night but as the only light was provided by our candles we could not work out where they came from. We discovered from their footprints in the morning dew that our visitors had been a troop of hippos. We never saw the Mountains of the Moon – they were buried in cloud – but we met some friendly pygmies, who seemed most interested in us.

Before Marye left us for home, we were invited yet again to Government House in Nairobi, this time to a party for the Prince of Wales. Marye and I, being about the only unmarried young females around at that time were, I suppose, a welcome addition. Also staying were Baron and Baroness Blixen (the authoress Isak Dinesen), Lord and Lady Delamere, Denys Finch Hatton (a famous white hunter), Titch Miles and his sister Dolly and my uncle and aunt. Only Dolly, Marye and myself remain alive. The Prince was staying there a few days before going on safari. He objected strongly to the rule that he should always be accompanied by a doctor, and this caused some worry amongst those

[75]

responsible for the expedition. In the end, unknown to him, Dr Bainbridge, an eminent Nairobi doctor, was sent along disguised as the driver of the royal car.

It was not long, sadly, before Marye had to leave, as she was expected back in England shortly. I wanted to go to Zanzibar and so did she, so we decided to combine a trip to the Sultanate with her homeward voyage. It did not sound too difficult to arrange. 'You can always get a ship from Mombasa to Zanzibar and back,' somebody said. 'You just go to the booking office in Mombasa.' We went, and were told, on the contrary, that the only ship due to sail for Zanzibar in the immediate future was a Japanese cargo boat. 'Is that all right?' we asked anxiously. Oh yes, they assured us. It only took six passengers, but it was clean and comfortable. You embarked at five in the afternoon and arrived in Zanzibar by nine the following morning. Once on board we were rather surprised to find that that the dining room was shared with the crew, and consisted of a long room in the middle of the ship with a huge table down the middle and three passengers' cabins giving on to it from along each side. The crew were very polite but giggled uncontrollably at everything we said, and with each lurch of the ship throughout the night our doors embarrassingly swung open to reveal our cabins to anyone who might still be at the table.

In Zanzibar we stayed with a Mr Battiscombe and attended a dinner and dance for the Sultan's birthday. The Sultan was a charming old man, and very pleased to see us because it gave him a chance to return the hospitality he had received from my family on his trips to England. He had even been up to the Borders, where he had been given a grand tour by Walter including an inspection of the Buccleuch's pack of fox-hounds in the hunt kennels at St Boswell's. It was both odd and comforting to speak of such homely things in such an exotic place. Next day he most courteously accompanied us on a tour of the island and I made a pilgrimage of my own to see a memorial plaque in honour of my uncle, Dick Bridgeman, who had died there while on duty with the Navy in the First War. He had been in an engagement with the German battleship *Koenigsberg*, which had taken refuge in a

Tanganyikan river. We also discovered, somewhat to our relief, that the P & O line on which Marye had booked her passage home, conveniently included Zanzibar in its itinerary, so there was no need for us to take our lives in our hands on foreign cargo boats if we were to see Kenya again. At Mombasa we said goodbye, and I returned on my own to Deloraine.

8

I STAYED ON for over a year. Kenya was a wonderful period of freedom for me. It was a remarkable relief to be able to do and wear more or less exactly what I liked. I revelled in being able to dress informally most of the time, in trousers, mosquito boots and cotton check shirts, and be at the farm one minute and off in my car on some adventure the next. I suppose I was a kind of pre-beatnik, but I also thrived on the responsibility; responsibility not just for myself but also, to an important extent, for my uncle and aunt. As Aunt Eileen was first ill and then absent in England putting the children into boarding-school, I was left to look after Uncle Francis; and since he too was frequently in Nairobi on government business I was also often the ultimate authority in the day-to-day running of Deloraine as well. I have never been happier, and look back on this episode in my life as the greatest possible piece of good fortune.

I was sad to say 'goodbye' to Marye. We had had such good fun together laughing about all the odd things that seemed perpetually to happen. What with our visits to Nairobi and to kind settlers who had invited us to look in on them, I had by then made many acquaintances. Polo at Njoro, some fifteen miles away, was a popular excuse for people to foregather on a Sunday, and teams would arrive from quite a distance away. Uncle Francis was a keen player and, in spite of his badly wounded leg, a very good one. I made many friends and happily accepted mounts for hunting and gymkhanas. The atmosphere was delightfully happy-go-lucky. A man who lived about twenty-five miles from the polo ground would unharness his ponies after a match, give them a smack and trust them to find their own way home.

One rather boring young man turned up regularly at these events and kept asking me to visit his farm. After my making one excuse after another he eventually said he was organizing a tennis tournament and hoped I would take part. Being fond of the game and quite a good player I thought it would be fun and accepted. When the day arrived I set off with racquet and shoes, telling my aunt not to worry if I did not return till after dark. My tiresome friend greeted me warmly and I looked around for the other players and their cars – but there was no sign of either! 'Oh dear, have I arrived too early?' I asked politely. Looking rather embarrassed he said that no one else was coming and that actually he had not got a tennis court. I could not help laughing as it was such a silly situation. He offered to show me round the farm, to which I said 'no thanks' but suggested that some lunch would be appreciated if he had any? After that I took my departure, agreeing with those who had told me that some rather odd people lived in Kenya. Meanwhile my uncle, arriving back at Deloraine, had asked where I was. When my aunt told him he flew into a rage and said, 'But the damn fellow hasn't got a tennis court!' I heard later that when he next met the unfortunate man he told him what he thought of him.

That summer I made another visit to the Ridleys at Kapsiliat, this time for their local race meeting and gymkhana. Kapsiliat was one of the happiest and most beautiful of all the homesteads. The Ridleys had started from scratch, searching the country for a beautiful spot, cutting down the bush and building the long rambling house bit by bit over the years. It was surrounded by a lovely garden and lawns, with a few large and beautiful trees dotted around, a fast-flowing river full of trout half a mile away and, in later years, a dam which made a lovely lake, also full of trout. In the distance were forests of cedar trees and beyond that the Cherangani Hills – home of the ghostly 'Nandi bear', a strange and terrifying beast seen only after dark and greatly feared by the natives.

Mervyn Ridley had polo ponies and race horses, both at his guests' disposal to use as hacks for early morning rides before breakfast. The whole house party would get up at 6.30, choose their mount and set off in whatever direction they preferred. What could be more enjoyable? Mervyn and Sybil were the greatest friends of my uncle and aunt and of myself also, and it was a sad day when this happy home had to be handed back to the Africans. Luckily the Ridleys had died by then. My cousin, Pamela Scott, who lives in Kenya, went up to Kapsiliat not long ago to look at their graves. The house was falling down, the trees cut down by people who do not realise that with no trees there will come no rain, and just a few underfed cattle were left to search for food in the scrub all around. Alas, such is the fate of so many loved and beautiful homes. I cannot help feeling those European owners had a far deeper affection for the country than do the Africans today, who for the most part have no knowledge of anywhere else and just take it all for granted.

Later that summer I went to a very different part of Kenya to stay for a few enjoyable weeks in a 'banda' just south of Mombasa. At low tide the coral reef stretched quite a distance and one could wander about looking into little pools filled with small brightly-coloured fish. There were few people and the only buildings were the three or four open-sided bandas. It is now a popular holiday resort and houses stretch for miles both to the south and up beyond Mombasa Island to the North. The most famous inhabitant at that time was a hundred-year-old tortoise. Everyone going to Mombasa would have a look at it and be photographed sitting on its back. I read some years later that it had died – apparently it went to get some shade beneath a large lorry and was crushed to death when the driver resumed his journey.

After we returned up country we began preparations for a long safari through Tanganyika. Uncle Francis, together with Mervyn Ridley and others, owned a coffee plantation in the far south of the country on the borders of Nyasaland. We set off from

Nairobi where he had joined forces with the Ridleys, each in our own car and the African servants with tents and provisions in a lorry. The roads were even worse than those in Kenya and the rivers all had to be forded except the Ruaha, which was too large and deep to be waded, and accordingly boasted a bridge. The engine of the lorry broke down halfway through the journey and it had to be towed by me because my car was considered the most suitable for the job.

The first day of the expedition had taken us across the Serengeti Plain, today perhaps the world's most famous game reserve. It teemed with animals of all sorts, which did not seem unduly worried by our procession of cars and hardly bothered to look at us. Before crossing a district known as the Mbugwe Flats, we were stopped and the cars were sprayed to rid them of any tsetse fly, so as to prevent us carrying infection of the dreaded 'sleepy sickness' into that part of the country.

The inhabitants of the Flats lived with their animals in large, square, deeply dug-out houses – the thatched roofs being only about two feet above ground level. We paid a call on one of these strange, virtually subterranean dwellings. The owners were most friendly and kindly offered us a drink of goat's milk out of a cow's horn. We could not refuse and just managed to get down a mouthful, luckily with no disastrous after-effects. At another place I strayed away from our shady picnic spot and walked out of the bush into a village. The inhabitants took a horrified look at me and fled as one into the safety of their huts. It may well have been that they had never set eyes on a white person before and thought I was a leper or a ghost. I hastily withdrew to put their minds at ease.

Even in this remote part of the world we managed to contact a friend from the Borders – Billy Usher whom I had known since childhood. He had bought land near Tabora and his farm was doing well. We had arranged beforehand to meet at the local hotel. He asked if he could join us at our next camp near another farm in which Mervyn had an interest, and offered to drive me in his lorry to give my car a rest till we returned again to Tabora in two days time. To my dismay his lorry broke down, by fault or design I was never quite sure. Luckily after a while it got going again, and we joined up with the rest of the party well after midnight to find a very agitated uncle and aunt awaiting us.

We eventually reached the coffee plantation and had a relatively uneventful return trip. I managed to do quite a number of watercolour sketches during this expedition which I am so glad to have to remind me of it all. At Iringa, the southernmost town in Tanganyika, I was shown some beautiful life-size paintings of wild animals on the walls of the town hall. They were by a famous German animal painter who had been quartered there during the First World War. A few years ago at a State Dinner for Mr Nyerere, the President of Tanzania, I asked my Tanzanian neighbour if he had ever seen them. He expressed great surprise and said he had never heard of them, so maybe they were devoured by ants long ago.

Soon after our return to Kenya we attended a farewell dinner in Nairobi for the Governor and 'Joanie' Grigg, who had been so hospitable to Marye and me, and then travelled north again to help organise the first visit by a group of English schoolboys to the colony. The party of boys, about twelve in number, were put up by various families round about. At Deloraine we had the master in charge, who happened to be the son of the Dean of Windsor, and two of his pupils. When writing his name in the Visitors' Book at the end of his stay the master rather pompously wrote 'Windsor Castle' as his address. Much to his subsequent annoyance the boys, who quite rightly considered him something of a snob, added the initials 'S.S.' in front of it.

By this time I had made many friends and travelled around to visit them on their farms, in some cases to get some hunting, often just to lend a helping hand. My uncle had a race horse which he allowed me to exercise every morning. His trainer C. B. Clutterbuck – another well-known local character, widely referred to as 'Clutt' – had gallops about seven miles from Deloraine and I often used to ride over there to join in, invariably staying on afterwards to eat a hearty breakfast. There were three packs of hounds: one at Molo, only twelve miles from Deloraine, another in the Wanjoi (Happy Valley), and the third up beyond Nyeri.

It was to Molo I went most often. I had many friends there who were always willing to lend me a polo pony. It was lovely country, rather similar to the Wiltshire Downs, with rolling grass-covered hills and valleys. The altitude was 9,000 feet, and few Africans lived there because they found it too cold at night. The long, flat, Happy Valley at the end of the Aberdare range of mountains, was very different. There one galloped over rough scrub, rocks and pig-holes – a rather alarming experience, particularly as one knew there could be a lion lurking in the bushes. On one occasion I left the hunt to return home, realising that both I and the pony were too tired to go on. Passing a thick clump of bushes, my mount gave a terrified snort and burst into an uncontrollable gallop. I presume it had smelled a lion, an animal of which all horses seem to have an instinctive fear.

Once when staying in the Valley I joined some of the farmers in a hunt for a lion that had been killing cattle and frightening the natives. The party split into two: I and one other member staying near our camp, while the rest went farther afield. After this group had disappeared, a magnificent old lion stepped out of a cluster of bushes and stood looking in the direction they had gone. We shouted to try to call them back, but to no avail; so in the end we decided that on the count of three we would both have a shot at it ourselves. We fired, and the beast, obviously hit, staggered off into the nearby forest. The other party, hearing our shots, eventually returned, but it was decided to leave the animal for the time being and wait till the following day before hazarding a search.

Accordingly, at dawn we set off again, this time in line abreast. Unfortunately a light rain overnight had washed away any tracks there might have been. I crept along a vague path and suddenly to my horror noticed that my hand was covered in sticky blood. Wiping it off, I expected to find some nasty bite on my hand – but there was nothing to be seen. I then recollected that I had just pushed my way underneath a low branch and might have collected the blood by brushing against it. In other words, the wounded lion might be close at hand. I retraced my steps, and sure enough, the lower parts of the branch were covered with gore from where a bleeding animal had pushed underneath it. We never found the lion, but no more cattle were subsequently eaten.

I would never have shot at the lion had I not thought it might have been a cattle-eater. Contrary to popular legend there was not an excessive amount of game shooting in Kenya, especially by the white people who actually lived there. The original English settlers, like Lord Delamere and Mervyn Ridley, initially came to shoot, it is true; but they stayed to farm and so did their successors. They treasured the animals and grew to be very anti-shooting. They might go out with a gun to protect their crops or livestock or to get something for the pot or the dogs, but they heartily despised the trophy shooting of the big-game hunters.

Kenya may have been regarded as a den of iniquity, but the settlers on the whole were good and worthy people. It was just the few who used it as a bolt-hole to escape their creditors that gave it a bad name. The most extensive landowner was Lord Delamere, renowned for his unique distinction of being a blood-brother of the Masai; another legendary figure was Ewart Grogan, who had walked from Cairo to the Cape in order to persuade the girl he loved to marry him – which she did! Both these formidable characters took a leading part in the political life and welfare of the country.

Much gossip surrounded the settlers of Happy Valley, many of whom, however, were most respectable and serious farmers. Perhaps the most colourful of the settlers at that date were 'Boy' and Genessie Long, who set off their good looks with the most beautifully cut and carefully chosen clothes. 'Boy' invariably sported riding-boots and a very dashing sombrero trimmed with snakeskin. They had a magnificent estate overlooking Lake Nakura, now an attractive game park.

Here I met Evelyn Waugh, who had just arrived from the Coronation of Haile Selassie where Prince Henry had been, representing King George V. Although only in Kenya a few days Waugh had already succeeded in making himself very unpopular. He seemed to take a malicious pleasure in irritating people. One evening we had a picnic dinner. When the moon came out he put on a very conspicuous hat and announced: 'I'm told the Kenya moon is dangerous and makes people decidedly odd. I think I'd better keep my hat on.' During our stay the Longs and their near-neighbours suffered a great deal of damage from a huge grass fire. From the house we watched this inferno rage in the darkness. Although a beautiful and awe-inspiring sight, to many of the party it represented the loss of their most precious pasture, so its beauty was not for them a matter of the first concern. But Evelyn Waugh would not stop. 'Oh, what a wonderful sight!' he kept exclaiming. 'Isn't it magnificent?' The stony lack of response to his enthusiasm only spurred him to greater extravagance. It was all done on purpose to get a reaction, of course.

A character who was undeniably responsible for giving Kenya some of its reputation was Raymond de Trafford – a remarkable individual who was known to most people as 'The Borstal Boy'. He had suffered the indignity of being shot by his wife. Before I left for Africa everybody said: 'Beware of The Borstal Boy. Be sure to lock your door if he's around!' I never thought any more about this till one night, when staying with friends, a car drove up unexpectedly and in he walked. Having been waylaid by a sudden deluge he was looking for some dinner and a bed for the night.

The visitors' bedrooms were in a guest-house across the garden from the main building, as is normally the case in Kenya; and my hostess, while finding herself obliged to put him up, clearly felt somewhat uneasy on my behalf. I guessed that she had warned him 'to behave like a gentleman'. When bedtime arrived the two of us crossed the garden to our little guest-house. Sure enough, after a pause he called to me from his side of the door: 'It's awfully cold, isn't it!' I called back: 'I've got a rug in my car. Would you like it?' 'No thanks,' came the disappointed reply. I was slightly un-nerved by this so I crept to the door and tried to turn the key without him hearing, but it would not turn. 'It's no use trying to lock your door,' he said, 'because I know it doesn't work. Would you like me to come and push the chest-of-drawers up against it?' Over the following years I got to know Raymond

[85]

reasonably well and found he had a good side to him and was a well-read and amusing companion. He was one of those people who could not bring himself to stop gambling, but he was not in the least embarrassed at the resulting failure to pay his debts.

Christmas 1930 found me back at Kapsiliat – two more visitors' rooms newly added to the house – and the New Year once more at Government House, this time with the recently appointed Sir Henry and Lady Moore as our host and hostess.

It was the custom in Kenya to get up at about 6 a.m. so as to make the most of the day before the oppressive heat set in. At Deloraine I would often follow the game tracks up into the forest behind the farm, and thanks to this I soon made friends with one of the Kenyan forest tribes, the Wandarobo. One of this tribe, Arap Lesse, particularly befriended me and acted as my guide. He showed me buffalo and other animals I would never have seen otherwise, and even promised to take me to see the rarest of woodland antelopes, an animal called the bongo. Teddy Brook had always wanted to shoot a bongo, so I wrote and told him to come along. He was delighted at the idea and hurriedly made plans to get the necessary shooting permit. News of this greatly upset the head game warden, who hated people to go out on this kind of expedition unless he was along to help.

When the day arrived we set off on foot with Marslie Truman (a near neighbour) as chaperone and a dozen or more Africans to carry our camping equipment. Arap Lesse led us into the depths of the forest, where we pitched camp by a spring in an open glade. Early next morning we left Marslie to spend a peaceful day with her knitting and a rifle in case buffalo should appear, and started to climb another five or six hundred feet through thick forest to the high and remote area frequented by the bongo. The camp was already above 8,000 feet so the thinness of the air made the climb tiring, a difficulty not mitigated by the need to keep very quiet and not to tread heavily on the mass of dry twigs that littered our path.

At last we spied the bongo grazing amongst some bamboo. Teddy fired and down she went. We both felt triumphant but

[86]

also sad to see the death of such a rare and beautiful creature. Arap Lesse skinned the beast there and then; Teddy got his head and I the covers for two large photograph albums. Having secured his bongo Teddy soon returned home. In 1933, during my second stay, he and Prince Henry went big-game hunting in the Sudan, but they did not come on to Kenya. Prince Henry was never to visit the colony while I was there.

Later that Spring I, too, left for home, with Aunt Eileen and my two cousins. This time, according to my photograph album, we travelled in a French ship, but strangely I can remember nothing of the voyage. Perhaps living for a year and a half at a height of over 7,000 feet affects the memory! Early Spring was the best possible moment in which to return to England. Friends and relations seemed glad to see me and hear about 'darkest' Africa, as it was looked upon by many of them. I must have changed quite a bit, having gained self-confidence from the experience and a greater knowledge of people and their ways of living and thinking. I lost no time in going to visit my sisters and special friends, who thoughtfully gathered others whom they knew would like to renew my acquaintance. Soon it was time to move to Scotland for the summer holidays and the grouse shooting; also to Teddy at Kinmount for some hilarious parties.

Hearing that I had plans, on my return to Kenya, to make further expeditions to see wild animals in various remote districts, Teddy offered to lend me his cine camera – a novelty at that time. Needless to say it was a very welcome offer. I saw little of Prince Henry; he was busy soldiering at Tidworth and at the end of the summer got shingles followed by an operation for appendicitis. I saw him briefly while I was staying with Walter and his family at Eildon – he was with his brother Prince George, the Duke of Kent. They had friends in Kenya and were interested to have news of them.

Before leaving at the end of October I was bridesmaid to May Cambridge and Henry Abel Smith. For this I stayed with Princess Alice and the Earl of Athlone at Brantridge Park. The wedding took place in the village of Balcombe nearby. It was a great joy to see them all again and on such a happy occasion. I knew all the bridesmaids except Princess Ingrid of Sweden and Princess Sybilla of Coburg – both these charming people I was destined to meet again when they were respectively Queen of Denmark and Crown Princess of Sweden.

By now I felt more than ready to return to the carefree existence of Africa. This time I was careful to stock up with painting materials, having found great satisfaction experimenting with watercolour. Amongst my fellow passengers on board the ship were Lord Furness, with his son and daughter, who planned to go on a shooting safari beyond Isiolo in the Northern Frontier. Hearing of my cine camera, Lord Furness kindly asked me to join the party. When the time arrived I set off with my faithful Kimani, stopping a night at Thompson's Falls where some acquaintances of mine had started a small hotel. To my disappointment they had gone away for a week, leaving the place in the care of a young assistant. He was largely occupied in trying, rather unsuccessfully, to make some Christmas cards to send home; so I lent him a hand, producing my box of watercolours and painting sprigs of holly and Christmas trees on pieces of notepaper. He was most grateful for the help and I sometimes wonder if he is still alive and remembers that evening, and if the cards were appreciated.

I arrived safely at 'Campi Shampagne' as it was and still is known. This lovely camp site beneath several large flat-topped thorns, had been used on a previous occasion by Lord Furness and appropriately named. Besides the Furness family I found three friends of mine in the party. They all went shooting while I sketched or filmed – the scenery and colouring being perfect for sketching and two old rhino obligingly turned up to be filmed. I am sure the young Furness son hated shooting the animals and only did so to please his father. Ten years later he was killed in France, winning a posthumous VC. The daughter, however, evidently did enjoy it as she later ran off with the white hunter.

After the usual New Year festivities in Nairobi I went on another safari for several weeks down south – beautiful country then teeming with game of every kind, particularly near the

[88]

Amala or 'Mara' river, a permanent source of drinking water for the animals. As beyond Isiolo, one seldom saw another human being in this country except for an occasional native. Rich tourists, with loud voices and purple hair-dos, now float above the scene in balloons while the ground is thick with minibuses.

Back at Deloraine my friends the Binghams looked in one day with news that gold had been discovered near Kakamega, a district just north of Lake Victoria. They asked if I would like to join them and a friend of theirs who had 'pegged' a claim. Always ready for a new adventure, I accepted on the spot. To find the place proved more difficult than we had expected. When we asked locals the way they just roared with laughter and said: 'Ah! *Musungo ku-chimba*' Swahili for 'White man digging', evidently something they found amusing!

We eventually found a camp by the riverside, where we settled in amongst our fellow prospectors, one of whom turned out to be Raymond de Trafford. Before 'staking a claim' one had to pay a token fee for a piece of paper from the District Commissioner's office, on which were entered name, address and 'claim' number. Then all one had to do was to nail the paper to a post, stick it in the centre of the designated piece of ground and hope for the best. A friendly South African showed us how to toss the earth and gravel in a basin of water, chucking out the contents at intervals so that the pieces of gold, being heavier than the rest, would remain behind till the final shake. I found one small nugget.

While the Binghams went to Kisumo, a few hours' journey further on, to try to obtain an order for the cream and cheese they made on their farm, I and the friend went to investigate a claim belonging to a neighbour who had had to leave it to go away on farm business. It was in a small stream off the main river, and we struggled along on hands and knees as the undergrowth was thick and came down to a foot or so above the water. I went in front so as not to get branches flicking back into my face and, on rounding the final bend, came face to face with three astonished and rather angry looking men. 'What do you want?' one of them asked darkly. I explained that the claim belonged to a friend of mine. 'No longer,' replied another of the men, with a nasty

[89]

laugh. 'Our claim is pegged here now.' So that was that – for me it was just one more memorable experience. I paid another visit two years later and found a small town had sprung up. In the evening we went to dance at 'The Eldorado', a noisy saloon where the prospectors collected in the evenings. It was all very similar to a 'Wild West' film.

Being so happy in Kenya, I stayed till the middle of 1931 before finally dragging myself back to England. Even this journey proved an adventure. Imperial Airways had just inaugurated their flying-boat service to East Africa, and since it was a lot quicker and more exciting than going by ship, I booked myself on to the second ever flight; first, however, there was a two month delay because the plane broke down and then, only two days before we were due to leave, my pony put its foot in a pig-hole and I was thrown to the ground and broke my collar-bone.

The flight itself proved equally unlucky. Hardly had we left Uganda behind before we were forced to land on the Nile to avoid a dust storm. We could not sleep on the plane because of the danger of mosquitoes, so one of the local fishermen was persuaded to take us ashore in his wobbly, dug-out tree of a boat. We were then transported in the back of a lorry to the nearest mission-station. Carrying one arm in a sling had proved a great nuisance, and the uncalled-for activity had also painfully inflamed my shoulder, so I ripped off the bandaging and did without till we reached Khartoum. There the bone was re-set by a doctor whom I was to meet again when visiting a hospital during the war.

Home again, I decided to stay for quite a while and eventually remained till the autumn of 1933. Disapproving of my visits to Kenya, my father warned me that if I was determined to go again it would have to be at my own expense. This confronted me for the first time with the task of earning money, and I decided to hold an exhibition of my sketches. Painting was not something that I had done much before I went to Kenya, but when I got there I found myself taking it up simply because (this being before the days of colour photography) there was no other way of recording the colouring of the place. My sketching expeditions proved to be one of the most rewarding features of my Kenyan life – peaceful, instructive and full of incident.

Monkeys were particularly mischievous. Once I left my painting for a short time to take a stroll and returned to find one holding my brushes. He ran off chattering excitedly and climbed a tree – and that was the last I saw of them. They were at their worst and most excitable if one was with a dog, and it was not unknown for monkeys to jump down in a gang on such occasions, if they saw a dog unattended, and to attack and sometimes even kill it.

Another time I came face to face with a leopard. It was eating a buck it had just killed and looked at me with great surprise. I was not quite sure what to do, but decided to walk backwards, staring hard at it and whistling 'The Road to the Isles'. This display of sangfroid succeeded and he galloped away. Leopards too were known to go for dogs – it was even said that they would take one from inside a house, given the opportunity – but none of the animals had a reputation for attacking humans and it was never thought the slightest bit dangerous for me to go out alone.

I succeeded in fixing myself up with an exhibition of these Kenyan watercolours at Walker's Galleries in New Bond Street. I am sure the show met with much more kindly reviews than would be the case today. Even *The Times* gave me several column inches, including the compliment that: 'In Africa the artist seems to have risen to the occasion and, with imagination stimulated by unusual shapes and colours, produced a series of records which are interesting pictorially as well as from the topographical point of view.' I exhibited sixty-four pictures and sold 190 guineas-worth of them at an average of about five guineas a piece.

This was a great help to my finances. Only weeks before I had had to travel from London for a party in Dumfriesshire by overnight bus, simply because I could not afford to go by train. As it was my first time on such a coach, I was rather disconcerted when we stopped at intervals through the night at one pub or another. 'I don't think I'll bother to come out, thank you,' I told my neighbours, in answer to their anxious invitations. 'Oh, but you must!' they replied, looking at me in horror. I thought: 'Oh dear – something awful must happen if one doesn't get out,' so out I got; and joined them for large meals washed down with tea in the all-night cafés.

Owing to ill-health and the advice of her doctors, my Aunt Eileen decided to stay with her mother in England for a while. Her two daughters were by now settled at school in England. Uncle Francis had at last made up his mind to have his wounded leg amputated and was as yet still somewhat unsteady on its replacement. Knowing he would appreciate both my company and my help, and I myself longing to return yet again to that life of blissful content, I decided to go back to Kenya with him.

The money from the watercolour exhibition enabled me to pay for my passage and Billy gave me a further £30 with which to buy a tent, the ones at Deloraine all being very old and dilapidated. I went to Teddy Brook for his expert advice. 'Where can I get a nice tent for £30?' I asked. 'Leave it to me,' he said, and in due course a lovely tent arrived with a bill for £30. The first time I used this tent in Kenya it caused a great sensation.

'What a marvellous tent!' some authority exclaimed. 'I wish I could get one.'

'Why don't you?' I asked.

'Far too expensive,' he replied.

'Not at all,' I said with some satisfaction, 'it only costs £30.'

He laughed: 'Good Heavens – more like £300!'

And then I realised Teddy had asked the shop to send me a bill made out for £30 and paid the rest himself.

We went by flying-boat, a pleasant journey which should have taken only seven days from Athens to Kisumu. Each night we had to land and put up at the local hotel. At Khartoum the hotelier suggested that my uncle should spend the night in a new bungalow alongside, where there were no stairs to climb. Alas, things did not go to plan. Just before dinner the pilot came knocking at my door: 'Come quick! Your uncle has had an accident!' I rushed down to the bungalow and found that, in pulling himself out of the bath, he had grasped a china towel-rail which had snapped off and splintered, making a deep cut in his side. Luckily his cries for help had been answered by the time I arrived and a doctor was not long in coming.

Uncle Francis had to go into hospital for several days, and because the aeroplane only passed by on its southern journey once a week, there we had to remain. It was very hot. The town 'Major', an old acquaintance, came to my rescue and asked me to stay with him and his family in their bungalow with a bed on the roof. This proved to be far more cool and comfortable than anywhere indoors. Each morning I had a delightful ride before breakfast with the Governor's A.D.C. When the next plane arrived, however, there proved to be only one available seat. I was dismayed at the thought of being stuck in Khartoum for yet another week, but fortunately the pilot suggested that I could come along if I was prepared to take the place of the air stewardess. Naturally I was only too pleased to do this, so I arrived in Kisumu as a temporary employee of Imperial Airways.

When my uncle was attending the Legislative Council in Nairobi I was now left at Deloraine more or less in charge, aided, fortunately, by 'Loder', who stayed on as housekeeper. One of my worst moments came when it suddenly grew very dark at midday and, looking out, I saw clouds of smoke and a grass fire rapidly approaching from a mile or so away. Remembering instructions, I rang a bell to assemble the Africans. I told them to battle as best they could with the flames, while I dashed around opening gates and doors so that the animals could get out if need be. Luckily the wind changed and the fire turned before reaching the garden.

On another occasion it proved to be lucky that I was there. My uncle was due to return by car from Nairobi, and on that day a long drought ended suddenly and four inches of rain descended. I felt certain he would not attempt the journey in such weather, so did not sit up for him. Sometime after midnight, with rain still pelting down, his driver came hammering at my door: 'Please Memsahib, come and help. Bwana Lordi walking in the rain!' I dressed hurriedly and we went to put chains on my car tyres, warning Miss Loder of what was happening so that she could get some hot food and drinks ready. We set off, skidding from one side of the road to the other, and after some miles I was thankful to see Uncle Francis bravely hobbling towards us with the help of his faithful Ehru, the Masai servant. We were all soon safely back at Deloraine. I felt so happy to have been some real use to this brave and always cheerful uncle, for whom I had never ceased to feel the greatest admiration and affection.

My knowledge of First Aid, learnt while a Girl Guide and V.A.D. came in most useful. One morning the gardener arrived carrying his big toe which he had chopped off with a spade while making a bad shot at a clump of weeds. I shoved it on again and took him off with all speed to Nakuru Hospital where they fixed him up. He appeared quite unconcerned and obviously suffered little pain. Another time the 'Head Boy' (butler) arrived with bleeding fingers, having been bitten by a rat. The neat little criss-cross bandages I applied to each finger gave him immense satisfaction. He considered them extremely smart and decorative. When told they were needed no longer he went off looking disappointed. He returned before long, bringing a tearful child with bleeding fingers, obviously having suffered cuts from scissors or a knife. 'My son also bitten by rats and needs smart bandages,' he said hopefully. Needless to say I was much upset and cross with him, but still had to do the best I could to bind up the small fingers.

While my uncle was in Nairobi I went off visiting my many friends around the country, and for Christmas that year we both went again to the Ridleys at Kapsiliat. After Nairobi for the New Year festivities came a three week safari again to the Mara River with a party of friends. We covered a large area of this vast, uninhabited part of Kenya and Tanzania. There were no roads, except for occasional remains of tracks made by the game-wardens. We never came across another human soul, but there were hordes of animals of every variety. How different to the Game Park today, with innumerable tourists and minibuses, and the game rapidly decreasing.

While visiting friends at Nyeri we spent a night at 'Tree Tops', a wooden building perched out of animals' reach in a large fig tree overlooking a waterhole and salt-lick. Here rhino and other creatures came after sunset to drink and play around. It had only just been built, and I am sure the owner had no idea how popular it would turn out to be with tourists in the years to come. Our Queen and Prince Philip stayed the night there before hearing of the late King's death.

In trying to think of something else of interest that we might do, one of the party suggested we try to climb Mount Kenya, or at least get up to the snowline. Only a very few people had bothered or ventured to do this and it was really a rather mad idea for three women and one man to undertake. We set off from Nanyuki with two ponies and a guide borrowed from the brothers Hook (splendid characters known as 'Fish-hook' and 'Boat-hook') who ran the hotel. No road existed and it was a walk of twenty-one miles from the town to the snowline, climbing from 8,000 feet to 12,000 feet and often having to cut a track through the bamboo forest so as to gain a passage for the ponies. Our guide knew by some instinct where to go but he left us when we reached the upper edge of the forest. The Africans were very superstitious about the mountain. We camped the first night amongst the trees and the second at the margin of them, before struggling through rocks and bogs for a mile or two till we reached some caves below one of the peaks. It was snowing hard when we arrived and I have never felt so cold before or since; added to which I found it very painful to breathe for the first few hours. We could only just squeeze our four sleeping-bags into the largest of the caves. The wind whistled around making strange sounds and it was very ghostly.

Next morning we awoke to hot bright sunshine and I and one of the party set off on horseback alongside a small stream flowing down a valley between the two peaks. The ponies were surprised and mystified when we reached some quite deep snow. One night in the cave was more than enough, so we scrambled down to the shelter of the forest before darkness fell. I managed to take some good photographs, which pleased me. We were none the worse for this hazardous expedition, which shows how fit we must all have been.

Later that year my uncle and I set off for Uganda to see the Murchison Falls. Lady Moore went with us. She was the wife of Sir Henry Moore, the First Secretary to the Kenyan Government. They were later to be our host and hostess at Queen's House, Colombo, on our way to Australia in January 1945. It was a delightful drive across a large part of Kenya and Uganda to Butiaba on Lake Albert. From there we went by day in a small boat up the Nile almost to the foot of the Falls. We landed and scrambled along a rough path and a steep climb to overlook the top of the Falls – a truly awe-inspiring sight. Since that time I believe a road has been made and a bridge built just above the Falls. Uganda seemed such a happy country, with a friendly smile on every well-fed face. I don't think anyone bothered much about work but they appeared to exist happily in their own quiet way.

About this time an attractive Swedish film-star arrived in the country, causing no little excitement. My friend, who had organised the Mount Kenya expedition, was smitten and offered to take her on safari. She accepted with delight, though I doubt if she really had any intention of going. He proceeded to plan a visit to the Serengeti in Tanganyika, in conjunction with a friend who was a white-hunter, and invited me to complete the party. At the last minute, however, he telegraphed saying that the film-star had chucked. Could I find someone to take her place? There being no telephones and letters taking ages to be delivered, all I could do was to ask the girl who lived a few miles away. Though very nice she was extremely dull and about to become a missionary, hardly a substitute for a glamorous film-star! The men must have been sorely disappointed. However we had a happy safari nonetheless and took lots of good lion photos.

We called on the local game-warden who gave us advice on where to go. He was very fond of his lions and hated them being shot. A large notice near his house requested: 'Please try shouting before shooting'; a wise warning since people so often shot in self-defence, thinking a lion was about to attack them. In fact this actually very rarely happened. One day a length of rope attached to our lorry happened to slip off and trailed along behind. A lioness jumped up from under a bush and pounced on it, pulling and shaking it vigorously, whereupon one of her friends appeared to join in the fun. They tugged away for some while giving me, aboard the lorry, a good opportunity for a photo. This I later submitted for a prize in the Kodak International Photographic Competition and, much to my gratification, won a Diploma of Honour.

One night heavy rain fell, making progress very slow. We were determined to reach the Ngorogoro crater, which entailed a steep climb, but half-way up we stuck firmly in the mud. One of the party walked back to get help from a homestead we had noticed on the ascent. He returned with a young German who got out his tractor and kindly dragged us to the top of the ridge where we camped for the night. Next day we ventured on foot down into the crater, a vast area of many water-holes, teeming with game and bird-life. I am told there is now a good road and a comfortable hotel, so there will be many thousands of tourists who will have seen all this under less taxing circumstances. As for the film-star, she ran off and married Baron Blixen, Isak Dinesen's former husband, and that was the last I heard of her.

My next unusual experience was a 'riding safari' chosen by Susan Ridley for her birthday present. We travelled by car to a spot some twenty-five miles away, where we found our ponies awaiting us. From there we rode along a ridge of the Cherangani Hills, camping in the open at night. The scenery could not have been more beautiful, somewhat like English parkland – green grass, clumps of trees or flowering shrubs, masses of wild flowers – with a wonderful view over miles and miles of the Nandi Reserve. Buck and other small animals darted away at our approach. On our way home to Kapsiliat we descended through many native villages and habitations.

I was most flattered to be invited to join this novel expedition. Many years later my husband and I went again to this district for a picnic lunch, but this time by car. It was hard to find a shady tree to sit beneath; they and the flowering shrubs were no more and in their place stood untidy tin shacks and hordes of children, goats and chickens. The population had moved to higher ground and better soil.

Later that year I was persuaded by my family to go to India to visit my youngest brother George, who had recently joined the Tenth Royal Hussars at Lucknow. The family decided I was much nearer to India than any of them and it would be a good idea for some one to see how he was getting on. Owing to my elder brother Billy having previously been in the regiment, I had known many of the officers and their wives for several years. Captain Harvey and his wife wrote saying that they hoped so much I would go and stay with them and offering to put up a tent in their garden for me to sleep in. The whole idea sounded most attractive, so I booked a cheap three-month-return ticket from Mombasa to Bombay and set off to visit a new continent.

Amongst the passengers, who were mostly Indians or Goans, I discovered an extremely pleasant couple: an officer in the Indian Army and his South African wife who were returning from Natal where they had spent his leave. They invited me to stay with them in Peshawar, where they were stationed at that time, and offered to show me the surrounding places of interest and organise a hunt with the local hounds. Lord and Lady Brabourne met me in Bombay and took me to Government House for the night, putting me on the train for Lucknow the following day. I had a great welcome from my brother and his fellow-officers, many of whom had affectionate memories of Billy.

The tent in the garden was comfortable and I soon settled into the routine of Army life. A bicycle had been hired for my use, which I found helpful as it was the usual and most convenient means of getting around. Everybody had one. In my youth I had much enjoyed bicycling, so I took to it again with ease and even a certain enjoyment. As it was close on Christmas, great preparations were in progress for festivities of all kinds: polo matches, tattoos, dances and parties. At these one came in contact with the entire regiment and sometimes with the K.O.S.B.'s – the King's Own Scottish Borderers – who were stationed alongside. Friends in 'The Royals' would turn up occasionally for polo from their station at Meerut. Had my husband ever become Colonel of his regiment, as he had so much hoped to do, all this experience would have been of great help to me as his wife.

After Christmas, George went off to camp for three weeks and I, with a brother officer's sister, went to Delhi where we stayed with Lord Chetwode, the Commander-in-Chief, a greatly admired friend of my brother Billy. One of his A.D.C.s I had already met on the Griggs' staff at Government House, Nairobi; and the other I was to meet again on many occasions. They were more than kind and took us sightseeing to the Taj Mahal and other places of interest.

I found India a sad country compared to Kenya. You never saw a smile and the children seemed especially miserable and poverty-stricken, their eyes covered with flies. I was there at an awkward time, when Indians were beginning to agitate for independence and apt to be rude to English people. If you queued for a ticket or in a post office, the Indian ahead was inclined to go on with his business as long as possible, just so as to be annoying. They had recently for the first time been allowed to share railway-carriages with Europeans and when seeing one in a train they would crowd in so as to demonstrate their new equality, even though compartments to either side stood empty. It was all rather trying, particularly when they chewed and spat out betel-nut juice.

I said goodbye to Delhi and set off on my own again for Peshawar. More and more Indians crowded into my carriage as the journey advanced. I was thankful to reach my destination and to find my friends from the boat awaiting me. They had comfortable quarters but no spare room, so had fixed a camp-bed behind a screen in a corner of their spacious kitchen for my bedroom! They arranged expeditions for me to show me the district and places of interest. I was fascinated by the scenery and the wild, fierce-looking Pathan people. Potters moulded lovely bowls on the pavement and women wove gorgeous silk materials which were also for sale in the bazaars.

A dance took place one evening in the hotel, organised by the military – there were a lot of the Army quartered at Peshawar to quell the unrest which was always happening. I was talking to some Australian soldiers when two young Americans who were out there trying to sell cement, came and joined the party. They longed to see the Khyber Pass and look over into Afghanistan, but could not get the permission necessary to pass through what was known as 'Tribal Territory' – an area between Peshawar and the Pass, where unruly tribes were being a nuisance.

My army acquaintances knew a way through a wire-fence some distance off the main road and said they had friends at the Army Post at Landi Kotal on the borderline. They offered to take us along if we would like to go. This sounded exciting and we arranged to set off the following morning. My hostess when she heard of the plan, said she would like to join the party but on no account must her husband know of it.

We borrowed caps and woolly Afghan overcoats – with only our noses showing – hoping no one would stop us, for women were not allowed to enter the district. We got in by some secret overland route, only joining up with the main road once we were inside 'forbidden territory'. We then lunched with the army friends of the Australians and looked over the boundary-gate into Afghanistan, before undergoing a rather frightening drive back down the Kabul Pass, a road of terrifying corners bordered by sheer drops that followed the winding course of the Kabul River far below. Eventually we emerged by the same secret track as we had come in, safe and undetected. However, news of the escapade later got about and there was a great row. I had left by then, but I had already realised what a frightfully stupid thing it was to have done.

I went to visit General Alexander, who was at Rawalpindi, and then returned to Lucknow. There was already much talk of a great polo tournament due to be held by the Maharajah of Jaipur. The officers were anxious that George should be given leave so that he could be in the team. They said it all depended on me getting round the Commanding Officer – so I made myself pleasant to the Major and George got his leave. I was able to go because the dates happily fell just within the time limited imposed by my cheap return ticket to Kenya. The only misfortune, as things turned out, was that I bruised my leg painfully while jumping in the cavalry school's training-yard. My horse slipped and crushed my leg against a mud wall alongside the jump, and I did the injury no good by joining a pig-sticking expedition while in Jaipur. The stick itself was too heavy for me, and my attempt at one stage to catch the runaway horse of a thrown rider put an even more untimely strain on the injured leg. Of course in the general excitement I forgot all about it.

We had a wonderful week, dominated by the polo tournament. Several crack teams had been assembled, including one consisting of the Maharajah and his relatives, and others from America and France. The Maharajah was quite young but already had two wives. They were in purdah but I was allowed to visit them. One day there was a tiger shoot and we all had to spend the night at a magnificent camp out in the countryside. George and I shared a double tent with a partition. My bearer, who was like a nanny to me, said: 'Much better you have Lord's side of tent and he have yours.' This was for the benefit of midnight visitors! I never discovered whether George had any or not. The tiger shoot itself was horrible. The chief guest was a bogus Russian prince, Midvani of Georgia, who accordingly sat on the biggest elephant in the most comfortable seat. Hundreds of beaters then drove a poor tiger out of the bushes and everyone fired at it. One could not have missed.

My final days in India were spent with the Brabournes in Bombay, where Lord Brabourne was the Governor. Bernard Norfolk turned up at the same time, also waiting for the ship to Mombasa. He too had been shooting tigers and was now on his way to meet his cousin Bernard Howard (son of my parents' friend Lady Mabel Howard), to hunt big game in Kenya. Bernard's elder sister was my greatest friend and I had known him since he was a little boy. Everyone naturally assumed we had planned a romantic *rendezvous*!

Most of the passengers on our boat proved to be Indians and the only person we could place was a brother of Lady Furness, who was an Australian doctor. This discovery arose because the doctor, seeing me limping about, asked if he could be of any help. I showed him my leg, which by now was full of fluid, and he was horrified. He had no suitable equipment, but drained it as best he could with the aid of a fountain-pen and advised me to go straight to hospital on reaching Kenya. On the way the ship stopped at the Seychelles. Bernard and I disembarked and went to Government House to ask if we could borrow a car. The Governor lent us his, the only one on the island, and we drove to the end of the only road, a journey of nine miles. The following evening we landed at Mombasa. Bernard went off to join his cousin and I travelled north to Deloraine. The doctor was right. My leg kept me laid up in Nakuru Hospital for three weeks.

Not long after, bad news of my father's health arrived and I was summoned home. It was the spring of 1935, and I set out on Jubilee Day. When we landed at Jubah we got off and listened to the King's speech on a very bad wireless in the District Commissioner's office. Another Englishman had come over fifty miles out of the bush to listen – so there we sat, only just able to hear the far-off voice.

9

ALMOST AS SOON as I got back I went to stay with the Athlones for Ascot. Though nothing was said about it to me, of course, the idea was undoubtedly to put me in contact with Prince Henry again. Princess Alice probably knew Prince Henry was hoping to marry me – she was very fond of him and a good friend – and she was fond of me too, having got to know me in South Africa. So I met him there, and after that it was only a matter of three months till we announced our engagement. I had an instinct that one day we would marry and perhaps, without ever really admitting as much to myself, I went to Kenya for a last taste of freedom, before abandoning a truly private life for ever.

It was fairly obvious what his feelings were. He did not shower me with flowers because he did not do things that way – but every time I saw him I realised more clearly what he wanted. He was terribly shy, though, and I am afraid I made it no easier for him by pretending not to notice. I was busy meeting old friends and organising my second exhibition at the Walker Galleries but, after a while, we got in the habit of going for walks together in Richmond Park. He used to exercise his dogs there, and felt away from prying eyes. Then one day about breakfast time the telephone rang at 2 Grosvenor Place – luckily my brother answered. It was the Press. "What's this we hear about Lady Alice and Prince Henry?' they asked. 'First I've heard of it,' said Billy, pretending to be the footman, and this shook them off for a while.

Towards the end of the summer Prince Henry was posted to Catterick with his regiment, and I soon joined him in the north for a weekend party given by our old friend Teddy for the opening of the grouse season. That was when we became engaged. There was no formal declaration on his part, I think he just muttered it as an aside during one of our walks; nor was there any doubt about my acceptance. I was thirty-four, so I had had a very good innings. Apart from my great happiness in getting married, I felt too that it was time I did something more useful with my life.

After this my sister Mary arranged for me to stay with some great friends of hers – Lord and Lady Barnard – who lived at Raby Castle in easy distance of Catterick. Mary said I had a great friend at the Camp whom I should like to ask for dinner, so this too was fixed, but when I arrived Lord Barnard apologised, saying I would have to entertain my young friend alone, because he had to go out to attend a Boy Scouts' camp and Lady Barnard was away acting as hostess for her relative Lord Middleton, who was entertaining Queen Mary. He was mortified when he returned soon after dinner and found that my 'young friend' was Prince Henry.

Meanwhile Lady Barnard had mentioned to Queen Mary that I was staying at Raby, which gave her a hint that something was in the wind. Over the next few days we had a lovely time together, motoring around the neighbourhood, visiting the local antique shops to see if there was any furniture that might come in useful, and eating in sleepy country inns. The engagement was not yet announced and though people must have recognised him, nobody rang the Press or disturbed us in any way.

The next problem was, how to break the news to my father. He was so ill by then that we were worried about the effect the news might have on him, but when I did finally tell him he said he had guessed the whole thing for some time, and seemed much calmer than I was. He asked me if I was quite sure I felt equal to the task, because he knew how much I had enjoyed my independence. If I married Prince Henry I would have to accept that I was a servant of the Country.

Portrait by Cecil Beaton, 1935.

On the balcony at Buckingham Palace, 6 November, 1935:
(*left to right*) Princess Elizabeth, King George V, Princess Margaret Rose,
Prince Henry, self, Queen Mary.

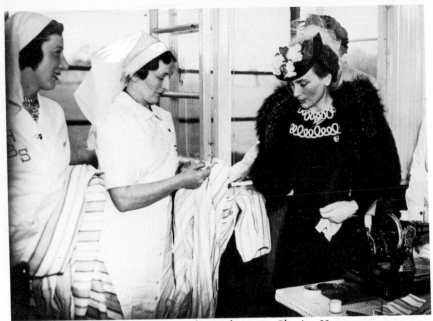

Inspecting garments at the Roehampton Clearing House
of the Central Hospital Supply Service, of which I was President, May 1940.

Richard's christening. From left to right seated in the front:
Lady Alexander, Princess Margaret Rose, Lady Sybil Phipps, The Queen,
self with Richard, Queen Mary, Princess Marie Louise, Princess Elizabeth.
Standing: Earl of Dalkieth, Duke of Buccleuch, The King, Prince Henry,
King George of the Hellenes, Marquess of Cambridge.
In front: Prince Michael, Princess Alexandra, Prince William.

With William and his late grandfather King George V's favourite pet, 'Charlotte', the parrot, 1941.

Holding Richard on our arrival in Sydney in 1945.

Commandant-in-Chief, Woman's Auxiliary Air Force, 1940.

'Sambo', a Christmas present of William's in 1946.
It was later known as 'William's Lamb' and its fleece was
auctioned annually with great success for charity.

Australia 1945-47: Prince Henry, Governor-General,
and I with koala bear.

Picnic at Norfolk Island, 1945. The whole population attended –
all 800 descendants of the 9 mutineers from 'The Bounty'
that had founded the colony.

The task has indeed proved more arduous than I thought it would be then, but no one could have foreseen the enormous changes that would take place: the extraordinary increase of publicity, the security requirements (at Barnwell now the house and gardens are filled with electronic eyes and a police-guard is on twenty-four hour duty), the variety of roles that royalty is expected to perform. Before the War a fair proportion of the official functions of today's Royal Family was shouldered by local dignitaries. Today such people have far less time and money, and this support no longer exists.

Members of the Royal Family too have to do much more for themselves than was previously the case. I do many things in the way of daily household management that, in my youth, other people – butlers, secretaries or housekeepers – would have done for me. My son and daughter-in-law, the present Duke and Duchess of Gloucester work as hard as we ever did – and incomparably harder than we did before the War – but they cannot afford a chauffeur, a lady's maid or a valet. We have to share such help as best as we can, and for much of his day-to-day business the Duke dodges about London on a motorbike.

The King was greatly pleased with the engagement. On 25 August, 1935, he wrote to my father from Balmoral:

'My dear John
    I must send you a line to say how delighted the Queen and I are that my son Henry is engaged to be married to your third daughter Alice. When I met you at Lords the other day I should have liked to have mentioned the subject, but there were too many people in the room. I trust you have given your consent. Our families have known each other for so many generations now, that it gives me great pleasure to think that they will be more closely connected still. I have not met your daughter yet, but hope to do so soon & I am sure I shall find her charming, she will certainly receive a warm welcome from my family. I suppose, if you approve, the official announcement ought to be made soon, but I wanted to see my son first, I hope this week. I am so sorry to hear

[105]

about your operation, I trust you are feeling better now &
more comfortable & will soon be able to go to Bowhill &
get out of the heat of London, which you must be finding
very trying. There are a few grouse here, but not very
many.

With kind messages to the Duchess

Believe me
yr sincere of friend [*sic*]
G.R.I.'

My mother and I were soon invited to Balmoral, I having
borrowed some suitable clothes from Angela. On the very first
morning I found myself sitting next to the King at breakfast.

'What are you doing today?' he asked.

'I'm going stalking,' I replied, thinking that as I had been asked
to stay with my fiancé it would naturally be assumed that I would
do whatever he was doing. I did not mean that I intended to shoot
myself, just that I would go with him. I could see the remark was
not a great success, and we exchanged no further conversation,
and off I went stalking with Prince Henry. I was a very good
walker so it was no effort to follow him. When I told him about
the effect my announcement had had on his father, he laughed. I
could not, it seemed, have made a worse *faux pas*. Ladies at
Balmoral at that time were not even allowed to watch the grouse
shooting, so the idea that I was intending to go out stalking was
completely beyond the pale. It later transpired that the King had
been so surprised he had not dared say anything.

The Court was much more formal in those days. One was
expected to change for tea and again for dinner, when one would
wear gloves and jewellery. Today only the most splendid state
occasions call for tiaras but at that time they were worn relatively
often. Such house parties as there were were not to the taste of the
Princes as the King and Queen invited very few guests and those
who did come consisted of old people such as Sister Agnes (a
Miss Cayzer), who was a particular favourite of the King and had
started a hospital for officers in World War I. The Princes were

also very much in awe of their father. He was very fond of them and they were devoted to him, but he used to bark now and then, and nothing they did ever seemed quite good enough. Not surprisingly the Princes were always happiest staying away at places such as Drumlanrig.

Back in London I spent a good deal of time at Buckingham Palace so that the King could get to know me better. He was very ill then, but apparently I amused him. During dinner he was inclined to go to sleep, and as my stories used to make him laugh I was always placed next to him. He was kindly and rather absent-minded, not making much effort at conversation.

Queen Mary, having been such a close friend of both my grandmothers, was especially pleased with the engagement. She was glad to have another daughter, the Princess Royal being so far away in Yorkshire and the Duchess of York (now the Queen Mother) so busy. The Duchess of York and the future King George VI were always an immense support. I and my sisters had always been asked to the famous garden parties over the years. We got very little pleasure out of them but it would not have been at all the thing for us not to attend. To get round this problem we used to go in by the gate nearest to Grosvenor Place, hand over our invitation cards, and walk straight out again by the first gate down the wall.

Next we had to choose a date for the wedding. November 6 was selected and the church, Westminster Abbey. My father appeared to be a little better and they allowed him to move north to Bowhill, but in mid-October a message came that he had not much longer to live. The Prince of Wales very thoughtfully lent me his aeroplane and I flew up immediately with Mida. Father was already unconscious but the doctor asked if I would sit by the bed for a while and try to make him talk. He did seem to make a slight effort. Next day, 19 October, he died. He had cancer and had fought manfully against it, because he knew that if he lived for a certain period the family would not have to pay such a large sum of death duties. In this final endeavour he failed, and the full amount had to be delivered.

There was great consternation at his death, and much talk of the wedding being postponed; but since the King seemed no less likely to die, it was decided to go ahead, in the private chapel at Buckingham Palace rather than the public splendour of the Abbey. This suited the King very well, and I was only too glad not to have a grand wedding. Immediate members of our family and close friends were the only guests, to the disappointment of members of the Diplomatic Corps and many hundreds of others.

It was a misty, drizzly day. A coach came to Grosvenor Place and Walter drove with me to give me away. Press representation was nothing compared to what it would be today and we were not accompanied by a single detective, but the crowds were enormous. It was rather frightening the first time one realised one was the centre of the attention; however, one knew one had to go through with it and that was that. Today, perhaps, there is more reason to be fearful, but it does not prey on my mind at all. I am hardened. I have been through too many things in my life. In the face of a crowd you are helpless, so it is no use bothering. I suppose one should just be thankful people remain so interested.

The chapel at Buckingham Palace was bombed in the War and no longer exists, but it stood on the site of what is now the Queen's Gallery. After the ceremony the wedding breakfast went off happily, except that we could not get the sword to cut the cake, because the icing was so stiff. This visibly irritated the King. When we came on the balcony the Mall was thick with people for as far as one could see, and thousands more cheered us all the way as we travelled in an open coach to St Pancras. The Duke of Kent's recent foreign honeymoon had been considered too extravagant, so we were told to spend ours quietly in England. We could not think where to go, but finally settled on Boughton, which was not lived in at that time of year. There we did some hunting, much to Queen Mary's disapproval – she always considered it a highly undesirable sport – before travelling to Northern Ireland to stay with the Brookeboroughs for some woodcock shooting. Three days after the wedding I received the following letter from my new father-in-law:

'Dearest Alice

Just one line to thank you for your charming letter & to say how touched I was by yr kind words, especially those about finding a new father to take the place of the one that you have lost. I should love to try and take his place & I shall always do everything to try & help you. Nice to think that you & Harry are having a little quiet & rest after the very strenuous days you have been living. But I fear yr weather has been very bad. Here it has rained every day since you left. We go down to Sandringham on Monday, by then I hope it will have improved & we shall be able to have a few days shooting.

Wishing you every possible happiness
Ever yr devoted father-in-law
G.R.I.'

I began to write letters to the 1200 or so people and organisations who had been kind enough to give us presents. We had received so many lovely things: silver and splendid jewellery from the King and Queen, the various wedding cakes, a white ostrich-feather wrap from The Ostrich Farmers of South Africa and a Standard car which we felt we had to return to the donor. There were of course more modest but equally well-received gifts, like a single lace handkerchief and a pair of blue bedroom slippers. We were to receive a lot of presents in the years to come, many of them rather useless things like elephant tusks, which we hid away till the donor called and then fished out again so as not to give offence. The most lavish presentations were probably those made by shipping companies when one launched one of their ships. They seemed to have a tradition of always giving a piece of jewellery.

After the honeymoon we returned to the regiment at York. It turned out to be lucky that we did have the wedding when we did, because only three weeks later the Court was plunged into mourning by the death of Queen Maud of Norway, the King's sister; and as we were about to emerge from this observance, the King himself died, with all the unhappiness and confusion of the abdication to follow. In fact, if our marriage had been postponed, it would have proved extremely difficult for us to contrive another date. A brother officer lent us his house as a hunting headquarters, which meant that by the time we arrived at Sandringham for Christmas Prince Henry had broken his collar-bone.

There was an incident at tea one day that I have always remembered. In those days Prince Henry went everywhere with two little black Scotch terriers. They were not popular at Sandringham, because the King's dog did not like other dogs; so they had to be rather hidden away. One day, however, they somehow managed to appear at tea. Knowing this would upset the King, we hurriedly hid them under the table and told them to 'sit' – which they did, till the moment Princess Margaret appeared. She was only three or four at the time, and began to run round and round the table; whereupon one of the Scotties jumped out and bit her on the leg. Prince Henry managed to grab the dog and shove him back under the table before King George noticed; and Princess Margaret, also knowing that the dogs were not meant to be there, went very red in the face but never said a word, which was noble of her. She disappeared to have her leg doctored in the nursery, and soon returned none the worse for wear.

It was a rather sad Christmas, with the King ill and the Duke of Windsor away ski-ing in St Anton with Mrs Simpson. This was another reason why Prince Henry and I were discouraged from going abroad, because we had also had the idea of going ski-ing and there could have been the embarrassment of a meeting. But the chief anxiety was the King's health. After Christmas we returned to York and from there to London, where we had rooms at Buckingham Palace. Prince Henry was in bed with a very bad go of influenza when his father's health worsened, so he could not go to Sandringham; but I went, and was there when the King died. I came back with Queen Mary. On the drive through London from the station it was touching to see how people took off their hats and bowed for her as we passed. She was very upset but controlled as she always was. I had received a final letter from the King on 14 January:

My Dear Alice

Many thanks for yr letter. What you say about the servants especially the butler is very funny. I am glad they are not yours. I hope you will find the pavilion at Aldershot warm enough. After very wet & stormy weather, we have got nice bright frosty days (11° of frost) & they have been out shooting every day, unfortunately I don't yet feel fit enough to shoot & there is so much to shoot, last week in 5 days 5000 head. We have had various guests who come & go. The Gathorne-Hardy's are here now. Much to our regret George & Marina & their sweet baby left us this morning. Elizabeth is progressing, but very slowly & it may be some days before she can come here, as she is still so weak. Mary we expect next week for a few days.

With our love to you both

Always yr devoted Papa

G.R.I.

The paper is still edged in black, the envelope sealed with black wax, in mourning for Queen Maud. It was written six days before the King himself was to die.

The 'pavilion' was the Royal Pavilion at Aldershot, which was to be our home during Prince Henry's time at Staff College. Royal Pavilion was a large wooden bungalow built for Queen Victoria to stay in whenever she came down for her military reviews. The house was raised about a foot above the ground on wooden piles; if you lay down you could see right underneath. Once one of our heavier guests plonked himself down in a chair and one of the legs went straight through the floor. There were an enormous dining-room and drawing-room, a nice small sitting-room, main bedroom, bathroom, dressing-room and guest rooms in one of the wings. Staff quarters and kitchen were down the hill and connected to the house by a lift and passage; the food was sent up by this means and carried into the dining-room where it arrived none to hot.

There were several regiments at Aldershot – Guards regiments, Cavalry regiments – so we had lots of friends. We entertained and were entertained, and there were good stables where Prince Henry kept his horses and polo ponies. We used to ride in the evenings when he got home, and we also tried to improve the garden by cutting back the rhododendrons. I knew many of the officers through my brothers, so the life was one I found reassuringly familiar. I really had nothing much to do. A comptroller looked after the finances, equerries organised our daily life. I only had to order the meals.

In many ways my life was not much different to the one I had led before. We hunted with the local drag hounds, I watched Prince Henry playing polo, and for the Easter leave we stayed with friends of ours in Sutherland, the Paynters, where the Duke enjoyed fishing the Helmsdale for salmon. I was not so keen, having had more than enough of the sport as a girl. Being at home so much I had always been the one sent out at the last minute to get a salmon for the pot.

The change in my status did not worry me particularly. I found everyone bowing and curtsying rather embarrassing at first, but naturally I did not expect old friends in private to do such things or call me 'Ma'am'. Our official duties were negligible compared with what they were to become.

I was given no advice by anyone. I thought Prince Henry would tell me what to do, but if anything it was the other way round. He was a very vague sort of person, who hated any kind of fuss and bother, but was most particular in regard to correctness of dress or uniform worn at official occasions. He hated pomposity, and liked nothing better than the Army and an outdoor life. At Staff College it seemed he was destined for the command of his regiment, the 10th Hussars, and this was always his dearest hope. When he had 'homework' I helped him colour the maps. This did not escape the notice of his teachers; at the end of the course my handiwork was especially commended by the mark-giver!

Some of our most enjoyable visits at the time were to Welbeck, the home of the Duke and Duchess of Portland. One of their sons, Morven Bentinck, was a great friend of Prince Henry's. He also was very vague, but an outstanding musician. When on railway journeys he used to perch a board on his knee and pretend it was a keyboard. To the astonishment of the carriage he would then practice imaginary scales. One of his rare public performances was in the depths of winter at some charity concert. He always tended to have cold hands, so he secreted a little hand-warmer in his trouser pocket, filled with hot water. In his anxiety he had not quite fixed the stopper so, to his horror, while he was playing he suddenly heard an awful drip, drip on the floor and felt one of his legs slowly becoming waterlogged.

An annual and very popular event was the Aldershot Tattoo. This was a spectacular military performance which took place in a large arena quite close to the Royal Pavilion. What with rehearsals and several performances, we used to have to endure many noisy evenings but the Tattoo gave us a welcome excuse to invite friends to dine before attending the performance, either in the Grand Stand or occasionally wandering undetected behind the scenes watching the preparations and listening to the remarks of the performers – which were not always too polite. On one occasion when my husband had been asked to open the proceedings, the late Duke of Kent, when walking around the back, thought it would be fun to cut off the electric light cable just as his brother got up to speak. Luckily he had second thoughts and refrained from doing so.

Edward VIII was often quite close by at Fort Belvedere with Mrs Simpson and they sometimes invited us over to dinner. This was awkward, as we were as unhappy with the liaison as the rest of the family, but as a brother Prince Henry felt obliged to go. Mrs Simpson was always charming and friendly and, being American, also a wonderful hostess. After dinner we would play vingt-et-un or rummy or watch a film. It was very informal and they were most loving together.

I happened to be staying with Queen Mary when the matter finally came to a head. The King suddenly appeared after dinner. There were just the Queen, the Princess Royal and myself there at the time. He was in a great state of agitation and asked his mother if I could leave the room as he had a very serious family matter to discuss. Queen Mary was discernibly angered by this request, but with many apologies she asked me to go, which of course I did. Afterwards the two of them came to fetch me. They were very upset. 'I'm so sorry,' the Queen apologised again. 'It was so rude of us sending you away, but David has told us some distressing news which you will know all about in due course.' It was not difficult to guess what it might be.

The Abdication promoted Prince Henry to the position of Regent Designate and – much to his disappointment – effectively put an end to any further pursuit of his professional career as a soldier. Nevertheless we stayed on through much of 1937 at the Royal Pavilion, while arrangements were made for us to move into York House, the Duke of Windsor's home before he became King. Queen Mary, as is well known, was keen on visiting interesting houses, and since she was quite close by in London or at Windsor, she would sometimes ask me to go with her. I much enjoyed these expeditions.

Another visitor to the Royal Pavilion was the Emperor of Ethiopia, Haile Selassie. He had recently arrived as an exile in England and been given a house in Bath. For political reasons the King did not want to offend Mussolini, the recent conqueror of Ethiopia, but he felt sorrow and sympathy for the Emperor and asked Prince Henry to pay his respects on his behalf. Prince Henry, seeing one of the princes and remembering him from his visit to the Imperial Coronation some years before, said: 'How your little son has grown.' This was interpreted and met with the answer: 'It's a habit little boys have.' Whereupon conversation more or less ceased. However, this did not prevent the Emperor coming to us, in due course, for lunch at Aldershot. Everything went well till a small cream cheese was offered as the conclusion to the meal. Haile Selassie, having no experience of such food, helped himself to the lot. He then waited to observe how it should be eaten, but since there was no more to be had this proved impossible. In the end we had the embarrassing task of telling him that, since cream cheese was such a rich dish, only a small portion was usually taken by each person.

Having a 'grace and favour' residence in London at York

House, we decided it was time to invest in a home of our own in the country. In 1938 we bought Barnwell Manor in Northamptonshire. Barnwell was a sixteenth century house, built near the remains of a Saxon castle now containing a tennis court, and had in fact been a part of the Boughton estate till my father sold it for some mysterious reason in 1912. It was bought by a Polish family and then later on by a rich couple called Captain and Mrs Cooper. They had amused themselves designing a Tudor room, a Chinese room and so on, each one more garish and unsuitable than the next. Eventually Captain Cooper went off to Kenya on safari, where he awoke one night with an excruciating tummy-ache. His lady friend said: 'Castor oil is the answer to everything. Take a swig of this,' but unfortunately the poor man had a burst appendix, so that was the end of him – and for his wife, the end of Barnwell.

In spite of the Coopers' bad taste, we liked the house immediately and its geographical position – near Boughton, in easy reach of several of the best English hunts and close by several friends with shooting estates, including my then brother-in-law David Burghley – could hardly have been more suited to our needs. We bought the buildings and four tenanted farms – for £37,000, the larger part of the money left to Prince Henry by his father.

Undoing the Coopers' decorations was an expensive and, because of the outbreak of War, drawn-out business; but it proved well worth it. When we went to Australia in 1945 we sold the tenanted part of the estate for £47,000, and over the years since our return have succeeded in buying up land round about to the equivalent pre-War extent of 5,000 acres. Perhaps the happiness Barnwell brought is best conveyed by the length of time some of our original staff stayed with us, most notably Mr Amos, who only retired to Kent in 1979, and Mr Prater, who travelled the world with us no less tirelessly as chauffeur and, though also now retired, is still on hand to help when needed.

1937 was a busy year, with the Coronation and a consequent increase in our official duties. I was made Commandant of the St John's Ambulance Association and Brigade, received the Freedom of Edinburgh and accepted my first patronages. One of these was for an organisation called 'Invalid Kitchens', which had been started by my godmother, Lady Carmichael. It involved kind ladies running a voluntary food service for elderly invalids – the forerunner of 'Meals on Wheels'. There were only three of these kitchens in the whole of London at that time.

I also succeeded the old Duke of Connaught as President of the Royal Academy of Music. The first time I attended their degree ceremony I found the room insufferably hot and stuffy, and yet there did not seem to be a single window open. I asked if it would be possible to have some air, whereupon there was a great gasp of relief – apparently they were shut only because the Duke had always insisted upon it. When I began, all but half-a-dozen of the students were girls, as if music was considered a rather sissy thing for a boy to do. Now the boys outnumber the girls.

In the autumn of 1938, perhaps as a result of this increase in my activities, I suffered a second miscarriage and the doctor ordered a complete rest. We decided to go to Kenya. Most of the trip was spent on safari. Prince Henry did not mind roughing it but, as he had always had people to do everything for him, he was used to everything being perfectly arranged by somebody else. When things went awry he tended to rely on me.

Our white-hunter was very upset because I refused to use my big-game licence, which had been given to me as a present but cost £200. He also disliked the fact that I could understand Swahili. If he did not want to do something he used to tell us, 'Oh, there's no water there' or, 'They say all the elephants have gone,' forgetting that I had the better of him through overhearing the true facts from the Africans. 'That's not what I understand,' I used to say frostily.

It was the time of Munich, and we were told before we left England that if War seemed imminent we would be cabled to return. Throughout the safari, therefore, we dreaded seeing the dust of an approaching car or motorbike – because in those days the country was empty and no vehicle, except one on the look out for us, would have been likely to be out in the bush. One day to our horror a cloud did approach and the fateful cable was delivered, but when we arrived back at Deloraine to pack we found another cable just arrived cancelling the first. To our joy, we could stay another fortnight.

On the way back to England we stopped off in Paris for one night to see the Windsors. It was Neville Chamberlain's idea, not ours. The Government were still undecided whether to assign the Duke an official role or not, and before reaching a conclusion they wanted some guidance in the form of public reaction in England to news of our visit. The Windsors took us out to dine in some smart restaurant. I did not feel in the least chic, with the red dust of Kenya hardly out of my hair, but the Duke and Duchess were more than kind. By today's standards there was virtually no Press interest; nevertheless some mention of the meeting did appear in the English papers and a lot of old ladies duly wrote furiously disapproving letters, which I found quite upsetting.

Nothing we ever did in the years to come was to prove as controversial as this exploratory visit to the Windsors, though one is always in receipt of a certain number of cranky letters. The worst of them seemed to come to an end with the finish of the War, though whether there was any connection or not I shall never know. Certainly begging letters have not increased with inflation or the recent rise in unemployment, nor insulting ones as a result of the troubles in Northern Ireland. People usually write because they have had a request refused or unanswered somewhere else. Sometimes little presents are sent and are always acknowledged and accepted with thanks.

The telephone too has inevitably increased the number of unwelcome callers, though most are cut off by my staff. After the War there was somebody with a Scotch voice forever ringing up. He was kept at bay till one summer in Scotland, when a temporary footman let him speak to me under the mistaken impression that it was my brother Billy. I was trapped. 'Oh,' said the caller, 'got you at last!', and then embarked on a long tale of woe about how he had been a merchant seaman who had fought throughout the War but never received his service medal.

'Oh dear, how very unfortunate,' I said, as sympathetically as possible. 'I'm sorry, but I suppose there must have been a certain number of people in the War who did things, and it's difficult to remember everybody. I'm sure we're all terribly grateful to you for the brave things you did.'

'Thank you,' he replied. 'Now I shall have peace of mind because I know a member of the Royal Family knows about me.'

And he never rang again. If only I had spoken to him at the outset, what a lot of trouble we should all have been spared. The Press can be equally persistent. If they succeed in getting through to me I do not put on a funny voice, I just say I am somebody else. It is useless to try to be too clever.

10

IN THE LAST DAYS of peace Prince Henry was much with the King. 'Harry and George have dined with me nearly every night,' he wrote to Queen Mary on 28 August. 'I have seen more of them in the last week than I have during the year.' On 30 August I wrote telling her that 'Harry went to the War Office with Bertie this afternoon and saw all sorts of interesting things.' Just what these things were, he was doubtless not at liberty to tell. Four days later War was declared.

We decided to return to Barnwell and on 10 September I wrote again to my mother-in-law with a description of the harvesting: 'It has been rather exhausting as the weather has been so close and "muggy". Harry and any available grooms, footmen, chauffeurs etc have been helping to load the wheat on to carts and to stack it. And Eva and various maids and myself have been putting the newly cut pieces into "stooks". We are covered with bites! From "harvest bugs" I suppose.' And I go on: 'I have been asked to have a Hospital Supply Depot here . . . Each village has a working party and we shall have to send them the materials and patterns from here and then collect the finished articles to pack up and send off.' In the coming five years I was to visit Hospital Supply Depots all over the country.

On 12 September Prince Henry was formally appointed Chief Liaison Officer, British Field Force, and two days later was on his way to a secret destination in France with Lord Gort, his Chief of

Staff and Commander-in-Chief of the British Expeditionary Force. He returned for a few days in November. The blackout was already in operation and one evening we delivered some top secret papers to the War Office. While Prince Henry handed these over in person I sat waiting in the back of our official car in the gloom outside. Suddenly Hore-Belisha, then Minister of War, came hurrying down the steps, took our car to be his official one and next minute found himself sitting on my lap. I do not know which of us got the bigger surprise. He retreated in a great fluster, and I was still giggling at the thought of it when Prince Henry came out. Apart from this leave and two others equally brief, Prince Henry was to be away till just before the fall of Dunkirk.

Within weeks of the Declaration of War, circumstances and attitudes had changed dramatically. On 16 September I wrote to Queen Mary reporting the loan of our horse-box as an ambulance and that 'numerous workmen still seem to wander in and out of the house finishing various jobs at their leisure . . . The War is made into an excuse for everything.' It was also considerably to increase the extent of my public duties. By 11 October I had already accepted the Presidency of the Hospital Supply Branch of the Red Cross to add to my responsibilities as Colonel-in-Chief of two regiments – The King's Own Scottish Borderers, and the Northamptonshire Regiment and Commandant of the St John's Ambulance Association and Brigade. In 1941 I was appointed Air Chief Commandant of the Women's Auxiliary Air Force (WAAF).

I was soon busy visiting first aid posts organised by the St John's Ambulance Association and later the WAAF at RAF stations; meanwhile trying to push through the modernisation and re-decoration of Barnwell, which was still barely habitable, though increasingly hampered in this work by the restraints of rationing and lack of workmen. Queen Mary had been moved for safety's sake from London to Badminton in the depths of the Gloucestershire countryside. Here, at the home of the Duke of Beaufort, she had a private suite of rooms, her own household and a platoon of soldiers as a bodyguard, but she still missed her life in London. She kept herself and the men busy by organising what she called her 'wooding', a daily session of clearing a wood near the house of undergrowth and unsightly timber, fallen and standing. 'I hope you and Eva will help with the gardening in old clothes!' she wrote, before I visited her for the first time that autumn. 'We have got far beyond the ivy, whole trees and shrubs came down in no time.' We maintained a weekly correspondence throughout the War and later when I went to Australia. It acts as a diary of that time, and all the quotations here have been taken from it.

I joined the King and Queen's family party at Sandringham for Christmas. Prince Henry was in France and Queen Mary was prevented from coming by a heavy cold, much to her disappointment. 'I hope you had a pleasant time and missed me a little,' she wrote plaintively on 27 December. I reassured her that we certainly had, and early in the New Year was rewarded with, 'I am glad you enjoyed Xmas at Sandringham: and missed me a little.' With my brother Billy as his ADC Prince Henry was occupied visiting our troops all over the north of France, narrowly missing death from enemy bombs on more than one occasion. It was therefore to my relief – though, as a solider, to his disappointment – that after Dunkirk he was withdrawn from the battle area. It was a grim period, though I was cheered up en route between some engagements when I stopped for lunch with Lord Lonsdale, an old friend, who was wearing his usual fanciful selection of clothes – extravagantly embroidered waistcoat, huge straw hat surmounting flowing white hair – and made his ponies and dogs go through their famous repertoire of tricks for my amusement.

When in London I stayed at Buckingham Palace. The King and Queen kindly gave us rooms when our official residence of York House was taken over by the Red Cross as a centre for packing P.O.W. parcels. One night Queen Wilhelmina arrived as a refugee from Holland. She had literally run from her palace in her nightgown and somehow been spirited on to a British warship and brought to London. There she was, a forlorn figure, in little more than a mackintosh, with not a possession to her name. That evening when the footman called in his customary way to ask whether I would prefer to dine alone or with the King and Queen, he added: 'Queen Wilhelmina may be joining Her Majesty, though only if a frock can be found for her to wear.' She was a rather large lady and none could be found to fit her.

A great fear concerning the royal family throughout the War was that the Germans would parachute in and kidnap us. Never, at any time, however, were we given instructions as to what to do in this event. The only innovation as far as I was concerned was the arrival, almost from the outset of War, of a detective – a Welshman soon nicknamed the 'faithful corgi' – who came with his family to live at Barnwell, and accompanied me everywhere I went for the next five years.

At Barnwell the male servants and employees were conscripted into the forces, so I was left with only old people who, nevertheless, manfully dug up the greater part of the garden and turned it over to potatoes. It was sad to see the flower beds that we had cherished destroyed in this way, but it was not a very serious sacrifice in the circumstances. My secretary kept rabbits, which meant that we were forever picking dandelions. At the height of the Battle of Britain I reported that our splendid neighbour, Lady Ethel Wickham, had given us a helping hand in shooting the partridges. 'It is wonderful that she can still tramp through the turnips at her age – I don't think she shot very many! But was better than *no* other gun!!' Lady Ethel was ninety at the time. In Victorian days she had been one of the best horsewomen and riders to hounds in England and rather frowned upon in consequence. Her father, Lord Huntly – sixty years of age at her birth – had fought at Waterloo and her grandfather danced with Marie Antoinette. She gave William a redwood tree to plant – 'metasequoia glyptostroboides' – because she thought it would be amusing for him in his old age to tell his grandchildren that it had been given to him by someone whose father had fought at Waterloo. It is apparently the fastest growing tree in the world and continues to flourish to the extent of three feet of growth a year. Other shots were also to the fore. On 1 November I pass on the news that my brother-in-law, Charles Phipps, 'who is over

50 is in charge of 16 anti-aircraft guns near Nottingham, which is really rather a good effort. He is a very slow and rather bad shot at pheasants but we hope perhaps he may find German aeroplanes easier to hit!'

My news on 12 November was more dramatic: 'Dearest Mama, I wonder if you have heard that York House had a bomb dropped just outside on Sunday night. It fell in Cleveland Road where there is now a huge crater actually touching the house. Marvellous to relate the house has suffered very little damage – it must be very strongly built and much more solid than we expected it to be. A piece of pavement about 2 feet square and 4 inches thick was flung into the 'Lady-in-Waiting's room' and landed on the writing-table. Needless to say there was not much left of the writing-table! Another huge jagged piece of concrete, rather larger than a football, landed in the spare bedroom. A water-main burst and flooded the courtyard and some of the basement. I believe masses of bits and pieces went shooting right over the house and landed in the courtyard. We both went to London yesterday as I had to visit the dentist amongst other things and Harry went to lunch with General Dill before going on to the Dover district – So we were greeted with the news of the bomb when we looked in at Y.H.!' We were eventually given a flat next to the Lansdowne Club, with an underground bomb shelter to which we could go when there was a raid. This shelter had been prepared for the King and Queen in the event of their having to abandon Buckingham Palace, and was therefore as secure and well-appointed as anything could be.

At Barnwell, in the summer, we had the first intimations that we would be required to take in evacuee children from London; and by the autumn they had arrived: two little boys in the main house, now largely habitable, and their sister with our butler West and his wife, who had a little house alongside. The boys stayed in the staff quarters. The cook helped to look after them most of the day and also my secretary, who with myself gave them exercise by playing cricket out on the lawn, and read to them before they were tucked in for the night. One morning they got up at four o'clock with the intention of walking back to

London; but luckily went in the wrong direction and soon got tired. When reprimanded they said the country was so dull and they wanted to see more of the raids and bombs. After a few months it was decided that it was safe enough for them to return home. Later, when there was renewed bombing, we had two more, from Islington. Thirty years later, when William was killed, the girl wrote a note of sympathy, so I replied and invited her to Barnwell for the day with her husband and several children. She remembered my maid, who was still with us, and recalled the little frock she had made for her out of a velvet curtain. Princess Alice, Countess of Athlone, was staying at the time and talked about her evacuees. I think the visit was a great success; certainly I enjoyed it.

My worst experience of bombing was being taken on a tour of Coventry two days after the notorious raid that destroyed much of the town, including the Cathedral. As we visited one factory, an air raid warning went off and the Lord Lieutenant of Warwickshire, who was taking us round, asked me if I would prefer to go to an underground shelter or to continue the tour. This was a very awkward question, but I hated shelters so I said I should much rather be bombed on the top than buried underground, so long as that did not prevent other people from taking refuge. 'Splendid!' he said. 'It will set a very good example to the workers. They're apt to dash to the shelters at the slightest excuse.' So we continued on our round and luckily no raid occurred. There was an awful communal grave they asked me to go and look at, where they had sadly had to bury hundreds of people anonymously.

Prince Henry and myself continued to keep up a busy schedule of tours and inspections, usually independently of each other. This could lead to anxieties, as when I reviewed some military manoeuvres that March by my regiment, the sixth KOSB's. 'An aeroplane came along and dropped out clouds of red smoke (some sort of sham gas) which luckily blew in the opposite direction and not over us! . . . In the afternoon they staged a very amusing sham fight in a little valley, which I believe the men all thoroughly enjoyed as they were allowed to use real bombs etc, which is not usually permitted. Shortly after I had left they were machine-gunned in one of the villages where I had been inspecting. When Harry returned to the Division HQ that evening a message was handed to the General to say that the unit had been machine-gunned, so Harry who knew that I was with them that day, got a horrid shock till he discovered by telephone that I had left an hour or more before it happened!'

A memorable exception to this division of our duties was when we both visited Belfast from 21–24 April, 1941. The visit, as usual on such occasions, was kept secret beforehand, and I had to wear uniform for the flight, so that if the plane was shot down and I fell into enemy hands I should be treated as a prisoner of war. It so happened that the city was bombed for the first time on the night of 20 April. It proved a great surprise because 'Lord Haw Haw' had said the Germans would never bomb Belfast, since they wanted the shipyards undamaged for when they themselves took over. Accordingly, no one had bothered much with air-raid precautions. The bombers had greatly increased the scale of the disaster by mistaking the glint of the city's reservoirs in the moonlight for the ship-building yards, thus dropping most of their bombs on residential areas. When we appeared the following day, it looked as if we had come in answer to the raid, and as a result we were given an extraordinarily, heartfelt, even hysterical, welcome. The hysteria was not surprising. The smell of the blown-up houses was terrible – rubbish burning, sewers broken – one could hardly breathe; and everybody's face was embedded with a peppering from the blasts. The people were so overwhelming in their welcome that the police decided it was safe to let us walk amongst the crowds, which they would never have allowed in less emotional circumstances. Visiting the hospitals, in particular, one noticed the inadequacy of the air-raid precautions: no sand bags or buckets, no netting or black-out paper over the windows. The newly blinded men were the most painful casualties to meet; and I was almost overcome with emotion myself when a young man, who had just lost his sight, would not let go when I took his hand. In another hospital an old man suffering from shell-shock had hysterics when a tactless cameraman took a flashlight photograph in his face as I was talking at the bedside.

May brought confirmation that I was again expecting a baby. On the 31st Queen Mary wrote: 'I was so thrilled and delighted at your good news this morning that I nearly fell off my dressing table stool in my excitement!' She was very exercised on my behalf with everything to do with the baby, and advises me on 22 July: 'Fortnum and Mason are *so expensive* that I think you had better go elsewhere for the cradle.' Just what part of the baby's layette could be bought with coupons and what without particularly troubled her.

'Do you know I think it is very difficult to order the layette in this tiresome way, I mean by letter,' she wrote me on 13 August, 'and you do not tell me how many you want of the various items, so I return you the stitchery school list, with the items marked with the one, two, three etc, and a separate list for you to put down, how many you require of each item, what kind of material and what length, and please *you* must *give* me all the material as I know the school will be unable to get what you require, and please *let* me have lace and trimmings – I enclose a cheque for £50 for the various things by the stitchery school, as well as for doing up of cots and baskets . . . I hope I have made myself clear.'

Alas, I clearly failed to rise to the occasion, because on 19 August the two months of plans were finally ditched: 'Dear Alice, Thank you for this morning's letter. After all, the complications of ordering what you want from the School of Stitchery beats me, so I am returning you the box of patterns and silk you sent me a few days ago (unopened) and will you please order from them direct . . .'

A couple of weeks before the birth there was another present forthcoming, this time with a rather different result. 'A kind South African Doctor had sent me a case of oranges but Lord Woolton will not allow me to have it! Harry is furious! A rather curt letter came from Lord W's secretary to say that no one is allowed to send presents weighing more than 2 lb (about 5 oranges) so he regrets I cannot have them.' All the various War time restrictions applied, of course, as much to the Royal Family

[126]

as anyone else – in this particular case perhaps a bit more so.

William was born on 18 December. His delighted father got compassionate leave over the days of his birth, but soon had to return to the 20th Armoured Brigade in Scotland where he was acting second in command to Brigadier Evelyn Fanshawe. On 9 February Queen Mary wrote sympathetically: 'It is a pity Harry is so far away from you at present as I know what a lot of things you want to settle, things which one cannot do alone without one's husband's valuable advice, besides which it is so nice to talk things over together, don't you think so? That is what I miss so dreadfully for Papa and I always talked and discussed things.' He was back in the south, however, for the christening, which duly took place at Windsor on 22 February. The Archbishop of Canterbury performed the ceremony and the names chosen were William Henry Andrew Frederick. The sponsors were the King, Queen Mary, Princess Helena Victoria, Lady Margaret Hawkins, Lord William Scott and Viscount Gort, who was unable to attend because of military commitments. Once more Prince Henry had to disappear to the north. 'What a pity Harry will miss 3 months of the baby's adorable baby days which one simply loves,' commiserated Queen Mary, 'especially the first one! You cannot think how Papa enjoyed our first baby (that naughty boy!!!) he was always in and out of the nursery.'

Prince Henry was even farther away throughout the summer on a diplomatic mission to the Near and Middle East and India, landing back on 4 August at one of the new American airforce bases close to Barnwell. He returned unexpectedly and as no one could decipher the coded notice of his arrival, beyond the fact that it clearly announced someone of considerable importance, and because Cary Grant was rumoured to be on his way to the base as a rear-gunner, the press gathered on the runway to scoop the first pictures of the famous film star on foreign service. When they saw Prince Henry emerge, therefore, they disappointedly said 'Oh, it's not him!' and had vanished before he put a foot on the tarmac.

We subsequently travelled to Drumlanrig for a shooting holiday and then, leaving William, went on for a visit to Balmoral.

The drive from Dumfriesshire up to Deeside proved a nightmare because of dense fog all the way. As I was sitting next to the King at dinner that night someone came and asked if he could take an important call. We were all left in silence at the table, each one of us, and particularly Queen Elizabeth, suspecting something awful had happened. The King came back and sat in silence. I could feel he was in deep distress and soon the Queen caught my eye, signalling me to rise with her and lead the ladies from the room. In the drawing room we all assumed that the news must be of Queen Mary's death, not imagining anything else more awful that could have happened. Then the Queen left us and came back with the King and told us that it was the Duke of Kent who had been killed – in an air crash earlier that day. We all travelled by special train to Windsor for the funeral, and then back again to Balmoral because there seemed nothing else to do. After a day or two, however, we returned to Drumlanrig for William and were jolted back into the routine practicalities of the present by the news that our chauffeur had got drunk and driven into a river with the Drumlanrig odd-job man. We then discovered that he had frequently been drunk in friends' houses but they had never liked to tell us.

From Barnwell on 23 September I complained that the 'weeds are terrible and our lawns all shaggy and unmown and the yew hedges covered with long whiskers! It makes one sad to see everything getting into such a state but it just cannot be helped.' But this did not put off visitors. On 11 October I report that 'I have just looked out of the window and seen about 50 or more Americans having their photograph taken against the old castle. Quite uninvited!' The Americans from the local aerodromes so enjoyed visiting the garden that soon we left it open for anyone to come and wander around. One fair-haired young airman particularly liked it, and over the months was accorded some privileges like picking himself strawberries if he felt inclined. He used to come over regularly for his strolls; so when one evening, as I was hurrying back to the house to give William his bath, it seemed quite in order when I heard him say 'Can I look around again?' I thought nothing particularly of it, even when I turned to

With the children in 1947 at Drumlanrig, prepared for rain.

Arriving at the Independence Garden Party in Kuala Lumpur
with the Paramount Ruler of Malaya.
Prince Henry is walking with the Prime Minister, Tunku Abdul Rahman.

reply and found no one there. 'That's odd,' I mused, 'I'm sure he said something,' but there was no time to look for him so I hurried on. Afterwards I heard that it was on this day that he had been shot down and killed on a bombing mission over Germany.

Meanwhile the baby prospered, almost too much for his grandmother's liking: 'So William is walking already,' she wrote on 30 November, 'much too soon, don't let him get bandy-legged!' In the new year of 1943 I confirm that he 'hardly ever cries which is such a blessing and is very good at amusing himself with bricks and a little toy on wheels made by our chauffeur's son, which he pulls along the floor; and he does not bother me to play with him all the time like some children.' Two months later 'he is always covered with bruises and scratches as he is very inquisitive and venturesome and will climb under and over and on to everything, usually in a hurry, and then trips over something and takes a crash! But he is very brave and never cries much – He loves animals and has no fear of them at all and gives carrots to the horses who put their heads right into the pram. We have a 3 weeks old bull calf and he runs into its stall and strokes and pats it.' In May we took him to see Queen Mary: 'We did all enjoy our week at Badminton so very much . . . William has put on a pound! And Harry suspects *he* has put on several pounds!!'

In September we also visited my mother at her new home of Branxholm, near Bowhill, where she had retired after the death of my father. Here, in old age, she continued to be as other-worldly as ever, telephoning Billy in a panic when her cheque book was finished because she thought it meant she had no more money left. She also became rather eccentric. When she opened her garden in the Spring she would pick bunches of daffodils at Bowhill, and then stick them in the ground back at Branxholm in the hope of making a better showing. As for the house itself, she added a very inappropriate conservatory as a sun-trap, which also served as a dining-room, even when it poured with rain. It rained throughout our visit and, since the weather-proofing of the glass was equally woe-begone, there we sat at every meal with one particularly persistent drip playing on Prince Henry's head.

In 1943 I was as busy as ever. Eva Sandford, my lady-in-waiting at the time, was appointed to the rank of flight-officer, otherwise security arrangements would have made it impossible for her to accompany me to aerodromes. For visiting first aid posts I wore the uniform of the St John's Ambulance Association and Brigade. First aid posts were usually in private houses. They acted as rallying posts for the local VAD's and St John's and also storage centres for medical supplies. Inevitably they tended to be run by old people. Old people too drove the ambulances and served in the Home Guard, which really was rather like it was portrayed in Prince Henry's favourite TV programme, 'Dad's Army'. People with pitchforks did tend to be on the look out for enemy agents dressed as nuns. But the fun kept up the morale. One WAAF station I visited was completely flooded just before my arrival, so they introduced some ducks into the sitting-room to cheer the place up for my benefit.

On another occasion, when inspecting a station at Lossiemouth, the commander turned to me after my tour was over and asked if I would mind if he showed me a local country house he hoped to commandeer for the WAAF in place of the prep school they were at present squeezed into. 'There's a very difficult old lady who owns it, but if she hears you've been and approved and asked for the house she might let us have it,' he explained. I agreed, knowing full well that arrangements for my visit had probably already been put in hand. We motored about a mile till we arrived at a rather grim house, with an avenue of dark yew trees and a reception by air force personnel on the front steps, one of whom said: 'I'm afraid old Miss Dunbar has appeared! She has not been seen for ages – she's usually bedridden – but I'm afraid she's got up.'

In the hall all the blinds were drawn and the place was lit by a gas-lamp, although outside it was broad daylight. Miss Dunbar, a tall old lady dressed head to foot in black, received me, exclaiming as if in recognition: 'Miss Hannah!' Everyone was aghast. The commander tactfully explained who I was, whereupon Miss Dunbar also looked aghast and I was hurried away to look at the house – a sinister experience, with the blinds having to be pulled up in every room to let in the light. In the end I decided the WAAF would do better staying in their crowded school. By the time we had finished seeing over the house the old lady had disappeared.

I went on to stay the night with an aunt in Nairn. When I told her of my strange experience of the afternoon she looked very intrigued: 'You must have met the mad Miss Dunbar. Nobody's seen her for years, but she's always supposed to know if anyone with Stuart blood is coming to the house, and then she appears.' And of course, through the Duke of Monmouth, the Scotts do have Stuart blood. The WAAF did take over the house, but did not stay long because they found it so haunted.

The air bases around Barnwell brought their own hazards. One day I was in my sitting-room when an aeroplane came over very low, making a dreadful noise and trailing smoke and flames. William was asleep in his pram on the lawn. Somebody at an upstairs window shouted: 'It'll be down in a minute, that plane!' I reached William just as the explosion of the crash occurred about a mile away, and the pram leapt out of my hands; but it remained upright and William did not wake. However, when Nanny went to fetch him later he asked: 'Is aeroplane all right?' Another time, when he was rolling about on a rug on the lawn, a plane passed between the house and the old sycamore tree that stands about sixty yards away, knocking a branch off; but amazingly the pilot succeeded in gaining height and flew on to its aerodrome.

The noise of the planes had a very noticeable effect on animals. At the beginning of the War all the hunters were commandeered for service in North Africa – a very sad moment – and we were left with two polo ponies, who both proved susceptible to the vibration of aircraft engines. If one of our planes passed overhead they paid no attention, but when a German one did they began to tremble and get fidgety. German engines made a different sound – anumb, anumb, anumb – and the ponies recognised this and associated it with danger. It was the same with the bull mastiff we had; he was terrified of German planes, wriggling under the bed or sofa as soon as he heard them coming. We were in the line of their raids to Coventry and the midland cities, and the shock waves of the bombs would set the pheasants crowing before we heard the bombs explode. We were too far away for the house to shake, but once a plane jettisoned three bombs quite near on its way back to Germany.

We had our casualties like everyone else.

'We are feeling very sad,' I wrote on 1 August, 1944, 'as our extremely nice reliable and capable farm-manager-worker and everything else has been killed in that ward of 7 people at the Moorfield Eye Hospital. He had a piece of shrapnel in his eye during the last war and has had to have it treated from time to time – It had got worse lately and he was anxious to have this treatment done between the haymaking and the harvest. He was dissatisfied with the doctor in Northampton who had treated him a year or two ago and was particularly anxious to see somebody really good in London. With much difficulty (and most unluckily as it happened) we arranged for him to get a bed at this hospital. The eye turned out to be worse than he ever suspected and instead of being there for a few days he had already been a week and then of all unlucky things this flying bomb went and crashed on the top of his ward. Harry is miserable and feels he should have dissuaded him from going to London.'

Our fear of being kidnapped remained to the end. Grounds for suspicion were increased by the reports that our cousin Lord Harewood was being held as a hostage in Colditz. Once William arrived it was always my greatest worry to know what to do with him if the moment came. I had a plan with a local farmer's wife that I would hurry across to her with him and that she would say he was her little grandchild and keep him till the War was over. We also made a shelter in the old castle near the house, though we realised that it would be unlikely to avail us much in the event of a real assault. We knew in our hearts that there really were no precautions to be taken that would be of much avail.

Like everyone else we tried to carry on as normal a life as circumstances allowed. In the sporadic moments that Prince Henry and I were together we found our greatest relaxation in going out and helping on the farm. Occasionally I would visit Queen Mary at Badminton, accompanying her to a little bookbinding shop she particularly liked in Bath, or in search of antiques, of which she had a great knowledge, especially when it concerned anything to do with the family. Otherwise we would be out 'wooding'. This she enjoyed very much, especially tugging away the ivy from the trunks of trees; then one day in the winter of 1943 a sad letter arrived from her saying that most of the wood had been blown down in a gale so that all her 'wooding' had been unnecessary. However she soon found a new wood and started off again with undiminished enthusiasm. 1943 brought news that I was expecting another baby and also that Prince Henry was to replace Lord Gowrie as Governor-General of Australia in the near future. Richard was born in August and duly christened Richard Alexander Walter George at Windsor.

11

IT WAS with mixed feelings that we set off for Australia – happy to be given such an important and responsible opportunity in representing King and Country, but sad too to be leaving our newly acquired home so soon. The prospect of such a long and hazardous journey with two young children was a worrying one.

Prince Henry and I went to London to say farewell to the King and Queen who, with Princess Marina, came to see us off at Euston Station. I am sure that they felt as anxious for our safety as we did ourselves. The children and nurses joined the train at a siding at some remote spot between Northampton and Rugby (as far as I remember there was not a house in sight). Our departure had to remain a deep secret and suspected by no one. It was a dark and foggy evening when we arrived to embark at Liverpool. Here we were met by our old friend Lord Derby, Lord Lieutenant of Lancashire, in an invalid chair, and my much-loved old aunt, Nellie Sefton. They too had been let in on the secret. We greeted each other and then hurried to the ship – William, very excited, leading the way hand in hand with the Captain, Aunt Nellie, carrying Richard in a basket, following on behind. She came aboard and stayed with us till the last minute. Our ship, the *Rimutaka*, belonged to the New Zealand Steamship Company. At that time she was the only passenger liner that had not been adapted as a troop carrier, and she was also the first to set sail for Australia and her homeland since the beginning of the War. The passengers consisted mostly of air force pilots, who had been wounded, and Australian and New Zealand wives and children wanting to get home.

The journey, bound to be dangerous till Gibraltar because of the continued presence of German submarines hiding around the Irish coast was not improved by heavy seas. On our second night out Prince Henry felt sea-sick and retired to his cabin; and Nanny brought me William, saying that if I could take charge of him she would be responsible for Richard, even if we had to take to the lifeboats. I told her that the ship's captain had already warned us that it would be quite pointless to take a baby in an open boat – should it come to that – because at that time of year they would be dead from exposure within minutes; so she said that in that case she would go down in the ship with Richard.

About eleven o'clock Commander Robertson looked in and warned me to be ready for anything and to put on my warmest clothes; and soon after that the ship gave a mighty lurch, sending everything flying from the cupboards and projecting a trunk on to my head which practically knocked me out. 'I don't like it,' said William in a small voice. Next morning we discovered that we had been rocked by a depth-charge used in our defence by one of the nine escort vessels, the frigate *Nyasaland*, which had detected and apparently sunk the enemy U-boat as we turned aside. Next day a hot water pipe burst in Richard's cabin just above his cot – but luckily most of the water went into the electric light bowl. I wrote my first report to Queen Mary on 19 December, the day after William's third birthday, as we passed through the Bay of Biscay.

'They have taken immense trouble to make our cabins comfortable and attractive and the nurseries are beautifully arranged – very nice carpets, chintzes etc. Even a tiny table and 4 chairs . . . Besides being in a gale I believe we were zigzagging and changing course all the time to avoid a U-boat which was pursuing us. Mercifully one of our own escort dealt with it successfully . . . I believe there were a lot of bangs but everything in the cabin was making such a noise I did not hear them. I told William in the morning that it was his birthday but he was too miserable to care and said sadly 'I don't want a birthday.' However he cheered up

[135]

later and the ship's company presented him with a lovely trolley and pull-car. Also a beautiful pink and white birthday cake. At one time we thought of postponing the birthday party but in the end decided to have it. We were kept busy holding on to the cups and plates that kept running about the table and no one was very hungry! (Too rough to write any more now!).'

The *Rimutaka* arrived at Gibraltar and the safety of the Mediterranean, by then under allied control. There we briefly disembarked and with William climbed 'the Rock' to feed the apes, before sailing on to Malta to have Christmas lunch and listen to the King's speech and then on again via the Suez Canal to Aden. Passing through the canal the ship was invaded by a swarm of locusts. We were all at lunch, but Richard happened to be on the top deck at the time and in care of the nursery-maid, who picked him up and fled to the nearest seaman's cabin without first consulting Nanny Lightbody. The latter considered this an unhappy breach of discipline!

We reached Aden on 2 January. As we approached, my maid revealed she had a nephew stationed there in the RAF; so we cabled the station commander and asked if the nephew could be given leave to meet his aunt on the quayside. However, much to her disappointment, he was nowhere to be seen when we arrived, so she went off with some other members of our staff to a local race meeting. No sooner had she gone than the nephew appeared and to his surprise bumped into his brother, who turned out to be serving on one of our escort ships, the cruiser *Euryalus*. A steward took them to the nursery cabin where they chatted to Nana and Richard, who were almost the only passengers left aboard. Nana suggested my maid's nephew should make his way to the nursery at Government House, Colombo, which explains how – when Lady Moore, the Governor's wife, came to show me the childrens' nurseries – there was a young rating happily installed. 'Do you have naval stewards?' I asked, rather surprised, as we continued our tour. 'No,' she replied, equally nonplussed. 'I've never seen him before!' However, Miss Eliot, as a result, at last met one of her nephews.

In Colombo the Moores gave us a reception at which they

insisted the children should put in an appearance. William, scrubbed and brushed, duly appeared in his party best at the top of the stairs where two *peons* or Ceylonese house servants came forward, each to take a hand. William got rather red in the face and looked worried but said nothing; however, when they let go of him at the foot of the staircase, he had a good look at his hands to make sure they were still the same colour. One of the peons laughed and said: 'The little prince does not know us black people, he thinks we are dirty.' Luckily they were much amused. Lord Mountbatten came to meet us and he and my husband had much news to exchange. He took us with William to a lovely beach some twenty miles away where we had a bathe and picnic.

Soon we were afloat – in hostile waters again, this time the enemy being the Japanese. Portholes had to be blacked-out and closed, smoking cigarettes on deck was equally banned after dark. The heat in the cabins at night was so appalling that the Captain allowed us to sling a hammock and erect a camp bed on the bridge, so that we could sleep out in the open. One of the watch got the fright of his life when he took a tremendous tumble over us in the black-out. Things could be just as turbulent by day: 'I am writing under much difficulty as everything is rolling about. The armchair with Harry inside it has just come sliding across the room together with a table of drinks and several other things and they all seem to have landed against the back of my chair!' Our escort dropped us as we came within a safe distance of Australia. There was great excitement when a demonstration of 'breeches' buoy' enabled Richard's emergency supply of baby food to be slung by cable from one of the escort vessels to *Rimutaka*; and even more when the two destroyers and *Euryalus*, with marine band playing and decks dressed, passed close by in farewell salute. Each ship's company gave three cheers and that of *Euryalus* an extra one for William. The Australian Navy then took us on.

Instead of waiting outside in a cool breeze before entering Sydney Harbour on the following morning, we were told to hurry into safety and berth in the dock at Woolamaloo. A Japanese submarine had been sighted in the vicinity. There we spent a hot and noisy night before stepping ashore at Man 'o War steps. After laying a wreath at the War Memorial we were taken on what seemed a roundabout route to Admiralty House – so roundabout that we were convinced the police had done it on purpose to give a better view of us to their friends! – there to enjoy a cool and peaceful lunch with Sir Winston and Lady Dugan. He had been acting as Governor-General since the departure of the Gowries. William was kept quiet with an orange – the first he had ever seen. We set off after lunch for our official headquarters in Canberra, the capital. The crowds when we left were huge, and as Prince Henry, who always liked to drive, edged the car through them for the first miles of our journey, we could clearly hear friendly cries of 'Good Old Scotland!' 'Good Old Henry!' 'Hello Dukie!' and many calls of 'Cooee!'. Even in Canberra the streets were lined with flag-waving enthusiasts when we arrived in darkness at 8.30 that evening.

Australia at that date was a country of seven million inhabitants. The roads were bad and dusty, with debris and broken-down cars dumped anywhere and numerous dead trees, that no one bothered to remove, marring the landscape. Later I came to see the attraction of the enormous spaces and to visit the varied and beautiful countryside. It is the enormous size of the country that can never be comprehended before you actually travel there. One evening Prince Henry brought this home to us by spreading a map of Australia over the map of Europe, demonstrating that its land mass swallowed up more or less everything from Ireland to beyond Moscow.

The War had caused the Americans to make a lot of temporary airstrips and this enabled us to travel the country – 67,000 miles of it – to a greater extent and certainly in a shorter time than probably anyone had ever done before. Possibly more than anyone since too, because after we left a lot of the more deserted strips reverted to their natural state of scrub and ant-heaps.

It is hard to believe now that Canberra was right out in the country among the sheep stations. We used to drive along the little country roads in a pony trap. Government House was two miles from Canberra, with a drive and some nice trees. What a change there has been since those days. Canberra now is a great city. Flyovers, subways and innumerable houses have long since submerged the immediate countryside, where we used to ride for miles amongst the sheep and cattle. Government House, however, remains relatively unchanged with its large garden and long drive. Throughout the country the bad, dusty roads have been replaced by motorways lined with prosperous houses or immaculate verges; the little coves and beaches stretching away north from Sydney, where we regularly enjoyed undisturbed picnics, have now been taken over by tourist hotels and villas for almost the entire length of the coast.

Australia, therefore, was a sleepier, more ramshackle place in 1944, though there were already signs of the modern, dynamic country it has since become. When we arrived the Australians were fed up with England. They could not believe that we literally did not have a man to spare to protect them against the Japanese, whom they expected to invade at any moment. A sense of disillusion was widespread. The Duke of Kent had been assigned the role of Governor-General, but his death and the war had forced Lord Gowrie to continue in office as Governor-General long past his appointed time. Through the fault of no one in particular, the residences did not meet the requirements of a more active Governor-General, with a young family, and full complement of diplomatic staff. Nor did the Australian bureaucracy have much experience of dealing with the greater demands of the occasion. At Government House, Canberra, we were shocked to find the rooms virtually bare of furniture, pictures and even light fixtures. 'Poor Nannie was aghast at the miserable nurseries awaiting her and the children,' I wrote on 19 February, '– No electric kettle, no frigidair, nothing we had asked for! The much talked of kitchenette consisted of a covered-in bath and minute sink, hardly big enough to wash a baby's bib, and a very small cupboard on the wall! The day nursery is rather small. Has bright yellow curtains, edged with bright blue, a linoleum floor which looks exactly like pressed beef with a few streaks of orange in it. There were two tables, much too big for the room, both with the sharpest possible points at the corners

[139]

. . . The house seems to be full of silver fish, mice and rats and I am constantly removing enormous spiders and dropping them out of the window.'

The exposed position of Government House meant that there always seemed to be a wind blowing – its temperature could change dramatically, from hot when blowing from the north to glacial cold from the Antarctic south. A hot wind blew for the official photograph taken a few days after our arrival, making it difficult for us to look our best. William ran around the garden pursued by a horde of fat photographers who became more and more desperate for breath. The children were a great help to us in our work, though. The Australians as a nation are very fond of children, and much of our success was undoubtedly due to the informality introduced by William and Richard. They provided a good excuse for us to invite young people to Government House without causing offence to civic dignitaries. When four Office of Work employees came to hang our pictures they took so long that eventually I went to investigate and found them doing somersaults in the passage with William!

If wind and lack of shelter were a nuisance, so were the flies, which were everywhere because of the sheep. As a protection against them prams had to be netted, and even the childrens' hats. I was also rather disconcerted by the number of poisonous snakes that were killed in the grounds during the first weeks of our occupation. This was a great worry, with William running about, not to mention the children of the chauffeur and the clerk, so on a friend's advice we got an Australian terrier. With a dog nosing about everywhere snakes made off, and also it dispensed with any need for the children to collect balls from under bushes and other places where the snakes liked to lurk. They were big, shiny-grey creatures. One did not see them often, though every-one assured us that there were a great many of them about.

Milk was another problem, being of poor quality and un-hygienic, so we bought our own cows. Till that time we had it boiled, which William found most distasteful. Richard could not stomach it at all, and had to go on Alasco while we waited for fresh supplies of Cow and Gate – a commodity that proved impossible to find in Australia. He was three months old at the time but the doctor advised us to feed him steak!

After an exhausting day at 'The Lady Gowrie Club', 'I was alone in my sitting room reading some report or something when I heard a noise behind the sofa and out ran a huge rat and sat up and looked at me! I hurled the booklet at it and it rushed across the room. I then decided to try and kill it and went off to get help. Some of the staff had gone to the cinema and the rest to bed. However I got Nannie and some implements from the house-maids' cupboard and we bravely started a hunt but were not nearly quick enough and the wretched thing always escaped us. In the meantime my maid had gone to Alec Robertson for help and he and Dick Wintour came limping along with sticks (in dressing gowns) and after an exciting chase Dick killed it . . . The door into my sitting room is made of glass which seems an odd idea. The rat kept trying to jump through the glass and we could not hit it for fear of breaking the glass!'

Conditions were no better at Admiralty House, the Gov-ernor's residence in Sydney. 'Everything in the kitchen was filthy and had not been cleaned since last in use and most of the things fell to bits when they *were* used.' My first letters elicited a comforting response from Queen Mary: 'Well do I know that inevitable answer, "Mr. So and So must be consulted", when-ever a Government Department is asked to carry out anything.'

Admiralty House stands close by the famous Sydney Harbour Bridge, with a magnificent view over the water. At first I used to wake with a start at the sound of the trains crossing the Bridge, because it was exactly the same noise as that of the buzz-bombs we had mercifully left behind us. Our dentist also had a wonder-ful view of the harbour from the window of his surgery, with some well-kept public gardens in the foreground. Unfortunately a group of passers-by caught a glimpse of Prince Henry entering one day for an appointment and as a result a large crowd of women were soon assembled outside the window, waving to him as he sat in the chair. It really did seem a rather excessive demonstration of loyalty.

Back at Canberra on 20 March I have slightly better news to

report: 'There are two good tennis courts here (now that we have destroyed the ant-heap we found on one when we arrived!). The rats are really dreadful. We have killed a great many but fear not nearly enough. Even at lunch-time in the dining room one frequently sees them. They come in through some air-conditioning places up near the ceiling and have a good look at us and then disappear again! I think we are managing to get rid of some of the silver fish, though I have already found several inside photo-frames.'

The early weeks were a period of much fitting of uniforms. As at home my personal responsibilities largely concerned the Red Cross and the Women's Auxiliary Air Force (in Australia, the W.A.A.F.). In addition I was to be installed as Commandant-in-Chief of the Australian Women's Land Army and Honorary Colonel of the Royal Australian Army Nursing Corps. Uniforms could be stiflingly hot, though it was unwise to travel anywhere without an overcoat in case the wind changed. A visit to the W.R.A.N.S. made me note in my diary that I envied them their 'open necks' in the heat. Our schedule throughout the two years we were in Australia tended to be hectic, made all the more tiring by the poor health we all suffered during our stay. I was only just recovering when I arrived, both from the effects of the War and the recent birth of Richard, and never had time to rest in the way I should have; Prince Henry scratched his leg swimming in 'the Islands' visiting troops and appeared to have poisoned his system as a result, and William soon began to suffer from what was diagnosed as nephritis. While Prince Henry was in 'the Islands', Prince Philip of Greece arrived in Sydney on naval duty and paid a call on Government House one morning. I took him to look at Prince Richard, who was in his pram on the lawn, and the baby was very surprised to find a bushy red beard peering at him. I always regret that I did not think of taking a photograph of them.

On April 9 we held an investiture in Perth – a busy day but by no means untypical. My diary reads:

'H. took salute at a parade on Esplanade – Victory Loan march. Took 40 minutes in boiling sun. Had Investiture at G.H. and talked afterwards with recipients and their families. After lunch planted a tree in the garden of G.H. Had a rest and then tea followed by visit to Anzac House. Had a great welcome and many songs etc. Dinner at G.H. and then Lord Mayor's reception in Town Hall.'

I confided to Queen Mary that 'the Secretary's wife had produced from somewhere various old newspaper photographs of our wedding and other occasions many years past and stuck them up on the wall. In one or two of them I happened to be wearing the *same* hat as I had on that afternoon! One that I had put away several years ago and then had slightly re-trimmed to take to Australia, thinking no one here would know it wasn't brand new. It really was too unlucky.'

My letters were passed on by Queen Mary to the King and by him to the rest of the family, so I tried to make them as full and as interesting as I could. There could, of course, be unforeseen complications: 'You can imagine our dismay and annoyance when an envelope arrived here today,' I wrote two months after our arrival, '(by sea) containing 37 letters from various members of our party, sent off to England from Ceylon! I enclose the one which should have gone to you. They apparently got to the Colonial Office in London and then were sent on here!'

At the outset Queen Mary had clearly hoped for an equally detailed account of our goings on from Prince Henry, but the amount of paperwork he already had to contend with did not leave him the time to drop her more than the occasional note as a supplement to my more lengthy correspondence. At first she used occasionally to hint that he might write more often, but soon she came to the sensible, though slightly unfairly stated, conclusion 'that as Harry writes so seldom and it bores him, it will be better for you and me that we should write to each other every week, so I will do so and if H. has anything *special* to say he can then write'. She was, of course, also able to keep an eye on us through press reports: 'I have never seen in any picture that you used some of those pretty parasols I gave you. I thought that in the great heat they would have been so useful. That is why I always use one, as one feels the sun so *much* less.'

[143]

The parasols were indeed very pretty, but too frail and old for the boisterous winds and sudden changes of the Australian climate: such as on one day at Canberra, when a rain-storm from the south and a sandstorm from the north began to pelt down together in the form of liquid mud. I did once take a parasol on a trip to a distant town. We flew there and when we returned to the aeroplane at the end of the visit my Lady-in-Waiting, whom I had entrusted with the precious article, found that it was missing from the place where she had left it. Several months later it arrived in a parcel, having been discovered by an architect rolled up in one of his plans. He had unwound this for some business purpose, only to reveal to the general wonderment a Fabergé silver-handled lady's parasol! The thief had obviously been forced to hide his loot in the first available place which, for some strange reason, happened to have been this architectural plan.

It was Prince Henry's intention to visit the capital of every state within the first six months of his tenure as Governor-General; and by VE Day in May, 1945, he had almost fulfilled his ambition. Thanks to two aeroplanes, a York and an Anson, being at our disposal, we had together visited New South Wales, Queensland, Victoria, Western Australia, South Australia and even Tasmania. When the War with Japan ended, we succeeded in visiting three state capitals on the same day. Everywhere we were handsomely rewarded by the sight of huge and enthusiastic crowds and much personal kindness and generosity. Meanwhile, in our private lives we had begun to settle down, our principal relaxations being riding, which Prince Henry now resumed enthusiastically, deck-tennis, tennis and picnics. After dinner in the evenings we played paper games or showed films, both feature-films and our own. Once we were planning to show a film to a group of nine admirals after dinner at Admiralty House, and so hired an electrician to remove the vast chandelier in the drawing room because it interfered with the projection. When he started to take it down he discovered that it had been hanging by a single wire. As it was normally suspended directly above the table on which we had tea every day we felt this discovery amounted to a lucky escape.

With Richard (present Duke of Gloucester) in front of
the old castle at Barnwell, our home in Northamptonshire, 1948.

Dressed for the coronation of Queen Elizabeth II, 2 June 1953.

The Queen visiting Barnwell, 1959.

Ill health was the chief cause of anxiety. William, in particular, had a disturbing middle-ear operation and then a kidney infection while Prince Henry and I were plagued with tooth problems. Even Miss Eliot, my maid, had gone to hospital after falling off a bicycle. Not surprisingly, however, the conclusion of the War made all personal worries seem trivial. 'After the (Thanksgiving) Service, to which I went in my car, had a very warm welcome from the crowds all to myself,' wrote Queen Mary with obvious satisfaction, though her return to London from exile at Badminton did arouse one regret. 'I am much looking forward to going "home", though in some ways I shall be sorry to leave this place, especially the "wooding" which I really enjoyed. Do you know we have actually cleared *111* acres in the 5 years and 8 months.'

One of the features of political life in Australia at this time was the number of labour disputes and strikes. One day I experienced a most bitter and frustrating consequence of this, when the Sydney dockers refused to load a huge consignment of Red Cross parcels bound for Australian prisoners-of-war in Japan, which had just capitulated. I was already in uniform on the point of leaving to witness this stirring event, when news came that a halt had been called, ostensibly because it was raining. My staff and I were appalled and immediately volunteered to load the ships ourselves, but were told that that would have the effect of making dockers strike everywhere else in support of their comrades in Sydney. Next day the rain had stopped and loading resumed.

I was advised not to go down to the docks because tempers were still running high, but I insisted and after meeting some of the Red Cross people I asked to speak to the foreman who had authorised the strike. He was called Drake and turned out to be a middle-aged, weather-beaten, grey-haired old boy. I told him how glad I was to see everyththing being loaded at last and remarked what rejoicing there would be when the parcels reached the prison camps. When this did not elicit much response, I asked him if he himself had any relations who had been imprisoned. Whereupon he drew himself up and answered fiercely: 'No. I am descended from Sir Francis Drake.' I was taken aback, and only realised too late that he had misunderstood me and thought I was suggesting that some of his ancestors must have been among the convicts deported to Australia in the old days.

I saw later a great many of the former prisoners-of-war. It was not their emaciation that haunted me, so much as their suffering from cramp and even paralysis. Many of them had been tied up for so long in contorted positions that they had been crippled for life.

With so many Scots settlers in Australia, it was not surprising for me to come across comforting associations with home. The old house keeper at Government House in Perth, Mrs Coventry, had once been a still-room maid at Dalkeith, and Sir Frederick and Lady McMaster actually had a property in northern New South Wales called Dalkeith, where we stayed for a welcome informal few days.

The railway lines in each state were of a different gauge, so that one had to change trains at every frontier. On our visit to Melbourne early in November to attend a series of victory parties and celebrations, we motored to Albury before entering the Victoria train: 'At 3 o'clock we left the cars and entered the train (Governor's coach). There was a large and smiling crowd on the platform – and it was very hot. The children were both thrilled with the train and the attendant produced some ice-creams which were much enjoyed by all including Richard! It was a slow train and it stopped at every little station. There were masses of children waiting at each station and they all came tearing along to our window and pressed their faces against it. William and Richard were much amused and waved energetically and banged their hands on the window, trying to hit off the hands of the children outside. This game seemed to give great amusement and delight to both sides! . . . Although the children went to bed early they did not sleep till about nine o'clock, because at each station the children called outside for William and woke him up – so he had to peep round the curtains at them.'

The Melbourne trip was in the way of being a 'pick-me-up',

especially for the children, but peaceful family outings proved hard to come by. On 29 November I report: 'Yesterday we had our first "Free Day" so took William off to visit "Phillip Island", 1½ hours by car and ½ hour by boat. An attractive place with koala bears, penguins, mutton birds and nice sandy beaches. We had hoped it would be very private but alas that seems impossible. News of our arrival had got around and the little pier where we landed was packed with people – including a mass of Dutch refugees from Java (rescued from the prison camps). We were soon surrounded by this throng and had to receive bouquets and shake hands with goodness knows who. Several police were there but as usual perfectly useless.'

William, needless to say, proved the star attraction wherever we went. Banner headlines in the 15 December issue of *The Australian Woman's Weekly* proclaimed him 'William the Conqueror, the travelling salesman of Britain' and continued: 'He has broken the ice at many official functions, for formality vanishes when a small boy enlivens the proceedings.

'Recently at a Girl Guide's Rally at Melbourne Government House he sat patiently for 20 minutes beside his mother, who gave the Guide Salute to the parade.

'Then he began to gather sand and gravel from the drive and made mud-pies on the dais . . .'

There were other impromptu moments. Thanks to a mistake at Government House, Lady Dugan and I arrived exactly one hour too early for a formal inspection of the Victoria League, to the consternation of all concerned. Another time, just as Prince Henry was conferring a knighthood on an old gentleman at an investiture, there was a tremendous noise of a scuffle and a mouse, hotly pursued by a tabby cat, shot across the parquet floor. Of course, everyone got the giggles, and the poor worthy receiving the honour – who was kneeling with his back to the company – blushed scarlet, obviously thinking his trousers must have split or something. Investitures seemed to encourage ludicrous incidents. At another a child, in the full view of every one, suddenly swallowed a marble. His mother, with great presence of mind, held him upside down till the marble dropped out.

On leaving Melbourne we visited Benalla before returning to Canberra. 'Heat and flies ghastly. About 102 by 11.30. We next went by car and stopped for a picnic lunch. Harry suddenly said to me, "What has happened to your face?" I looked in my mirror and saw it was the colour of blackcurrant fool *all over*!! Harry wore shorts and shirts *only*, of the Air Force uniform, the latter he took off at intervals while I dried his back with a bath towel. By the time we got to Shepperton it was over 105°. I began to doubt if I would survive! Eileen also was looking puce by then! However we all managed to get through the visit. I gulped down some iced orangeade, which gave me an awful pain but luckily after we left.

'We had to stop to get cool water for the car. They said it was 110° there. My dark glasses were red hot and burning my skin so I had to remove them. At last we got to the place where our aeroplane awaited us and were revived by hot tea. Canberra we found equally hot. Downstairs rooms luckily fairly cool but bedrooms and nurseries ghastly. The poor children together with Miss Horsey and Sandy had also had a dreadful motor drive. Nannie held a sponge to Richard's head most of the way. They stopped the car to let William get out and be sick, and he nearly trod on a snake coiled up on the side of the road. When we arrived we found no electric power for fans and no light allowed after nine o'clock. No electricity for cooking, frigidair, irons etc. (owing to strike in Sydney). Not helpful to people's tired and frayed nerves!

'It was too hot to sleep and one had to sit up at intervals to breath during the night. William coughed all night which turned out to be whooping cough and Richard cried most of the time. All Sunday there was the same burning hot wind so the only hope was to close all windows. The nurseries were unbearable so nurses and children retired to the spare bedrooms where it was slightly better. In the middle of all this we struggled with unpacking and getting off Christmas cards. Everybody became quite vague and idiotic.'

Christmas Day proved equally hard to bear: 'I was all dressed and ready for church yesterday and about to get into the car when

I suddenly collapsed! Admiral Bracegirdle [Official Secretary] was wishing me a Happy Xmas when I suddenly saw him a sort of mirage. I just had time to seize Miss Horsey by the arm and disappear into Harry's room alongside. Too silly – but I suppose the heat was too much or something.'

The Bracegirdles had given William a black lamb for Christmas, a rather hot and smelly present in that climate. It was known as Sambo and it used to trundle around on a lead getting bigger and bigger while we wondered what to do with it. When we left we gave it to a farm nearby and for several years after its fleece was shorn and publicly auctioned for the benefit of disabled soldiers and sailors. It was always known as 'Prince William's lamb' and under this title enjoyed considerable fame as a sheep.

12

IN OUR FIRST YEAR we concentrated on the capital cities. The second year we visited the country areas and Agricultural Shows – the sheep and cattle stations, the county towns. This was much more enjoyable. The year began well, too, with a restful and happy month-long holiday in Tasmania. It was a great relief to have a respite from official cares and constant publicity. We were lent a charming house near the beach at Devonport belonging to the Lane family, much respected in that town. We could not have been treated with greater courtesy by the local people. In the mornings we would find welcome presents such as baskets of strawberries and fresh cream at our garden gate, left there by well-wishers.

We made an expedition to a silver mine, miles from anywhere – leaving our car at Burnie and embarking in a taxi fitted with wheels to run along a narrow railway line. We trundled comfortable through lovely scenery full of giant tree ferns and over a bridge with no sides, a roaring river rushing along the gorge below us. The countryside reminded me much of Scotland, and the weather, though it could be warmer, was also somewhat similar, being wet and very variable. Things could be familiar: 'We were persuaded to attend the local race-meeting yesterday! It deluged with rain which was rather sad as the people were so longing to "show off" their Race Course and Meeting to us. We huddled together in a very rickety stand with the rain pouring in till they cancelled the meeting and then we went and had tea in a tent full of leaks!'

There were novelties too: 'We took a picnic at a delightful spot except for the leeches! Harry suddenly saw one trying to force its way through his trousers and later we found several stuck to the rugs we had been sitting on! We all examined ourselves somewhat nervously after this but luckily no leeches had managed actually to attach themselves to any of us.' And the inevitable holiday drama: 'On Monday we had our first real hot day without wind and after lunch we all motored off to a long sandy beach about four miles away, and everybody bathed and the sea was lovely and warm.

'Richard adores the water but William is very nervous of waves and rushes away every time one comes along. In consequence he never gets very far out! At the end of this perfect afternoon we had a slight catastrophe – the car which we had taken down to the beach stuck in some very loose shingle and refused to get up about two yards of shingly bank. Very worrying, as the tide was by then coming *in*! No amount of pushing did any good. So we all set to work putting down big stones and sticks etc to make a sort of track for it. William got very excited and in his efforts to help suddenly *threw* an enormous stone which unfortunately hit poor Eileen just behind the ear as she was getting up from placing something under the car wheel. She was knocked out, poor thing, for a while which was very upsetting. William was horrified and very upset. We eventually got a kind farmer (who lived nearby) to come with 3 fat horses and they pulled the car to firmer ground.'

The holiday over we returned to Canberra, where at the end of February I report that we have seen 'a very amusing coloured film – *Blithe Spirit* by Noel Coward. It was shown in aid of "Food for Britain". The name "Captain Bracegirdle" comes into it and caused merriment all round. Apparently Noel Coward was staying here while writing the play, and was so taken with the name that he asked if he might use it. We did not know of this beforehand so were completely taken by surprise.'

We were soon back into our official routine. In such a large country this called for a lot of flying, entailing early starts which was something I never much enjoyed. A lot of the trips were bumpy, once or twice we were caught in frightening storms, engines were known to fail, tyres to burst, so I always set off in a state of some trepidation. Already on 11 March, I am complaining that we have 'had a rather bumpy flight [to Bega, New South Wales] and the aerodrome which was only "a strip" on the top of a hill, was rather hard to find. Luckily it had another aeroplane sitting on it which helped us distinguish it from the rest of the country!'

There followed a much longer air journey, when Prince Henry undertook the first visit in the history of the Governor-Generalship to Norfolk Island – 1,000 miles out in the Pacific, midway between New Zealand and New Caledonia. This proved the most extraordinary of our many Australian experiences. A tiny island six miles long, it looked like a waterlily leaf in that vast expanse of sea as we made our descent just as the sun was beginning to set. It was so awesomely isolated that the Administrator's secretary, who acted as our hostess, admitted that she had cried herself to sleep every night for a week when she first arrived. I mailed an elaborate account of our visit as soon as we returned:

'I expect you will know the history of the inhabitants – The descendants of 9 mutineers of *The Bounty* and their Tahitian wives who were taken there from Pitcairn Island at the wish of Queen Victoria in 1856 or thereabouts, when the water supply was discovered to be inadequate for the number of people on the Island. During *this* war the New Zealanders made an aerodrome and 2,000 of them were defending it at one time in case the Japs should try and get it as a base . . . Looking down from the air the "run-way" seemed to occupy most of the Island! The population there is 800 counting the children – But they have over 900 horses! Everybody rides, old and young alike. . . .

'[Government House] is a rather sinister looking building built by the convicts (there was a convict settlement before the Pitcairn Islanders arrived). We bumped over the grass between horses and cows as there was no road! Also no garden, except for a few geranium bushes up against the house. All around were grue-some looking remains of tumbledown convict prisons and walls, hangman's gate and suchlike! All rather spooky in the setting sun! . . . We had a dinner party that evening – A very tight fit in the small dining room. Most of the people are rather peculiar looking – to us they talked very good but old fashioned English and amongst themselves they used a sort of patois, a mixture of English and some tribal language of their ancestors I suppose! The dinner was a very disorganised affair, some people were eating "the sweet" while others still had their fish plates in front of them. Husbands sat next to wives.

'The following morning we went for a swim, picking our way through the barbed wire to the beach, which made us think it would not have proved an insuperable defence had the Japanese invaded! And then we attended a grand official lunch. This took the form of a picnic, attended by the entire population, which the gentlemen of our party found very uncomfortable, not knowing whether they should face the tablecloth and food or sit with their backs to it. We sat on the grass under the pine trees that take their name from the Island. Sheets about 6 feet wide were put edge to edge on the ground in a long line. I should think it must have been at least 100 yards long. Every family brought different dishes of whatever they could manage. Luckily there was a certain amount of plain cold chicken and fruit salad amongst many terrible looking concoctions. They were so anxious we should sample their various peculiar island dishes made of sweet potatoes, bananas etc. All very sweet and stodgy and unattractive! We all sat on the ground as you will see in the photograph . . . They sang a very attractive grace . . . The whole thing was really rather touching – They were all so happy and excited. It was like an enormous family party, which in fact I suppose it was as practically all of the inhabitants are related to each other! They all seemed to be called Nobbs, Buffet or Christian – most confusing for the postman I believe.

'After this wonderful picnic we went to the races. One of them was won by the manservant at Government House and another by one of our waitresses! . . . Most of the islanders and school-

children came to see us off. They sang a hymn very beautifully
. . . Except for the aerodrome the whole thing was rather like
something out of a book of a hundred years ago. The inhabitants
call themselves English and are *very proud* of it and hate having to
belong to the Commonwealth of Australia! They have the most
tremendous veneration for Queen Victoria. Apparently women
who left Pitcairn Island were each given a little sewing case from
her and there are still some in existence that are greatly treasured.'

Disputes between communists and non-communists within
the various trade unions continued to cause strikes and unrest,
and when we toured the steel works at Port Kembla, New South
Wales, early in April, five communist union leaders decided to
boycott the visit. Everyone else received us kindly, however,
and the next day there was a friendly cartoon depicting one of the
disgruntled absentees saying to his comrades: 'But if we HAD
gone, nobody would have noticed us.'

The rest of the month I was plagued again with fevers, sore
throats and tummy pains and eventually underwent an appendix
operation which required me to be in the appropriately named
Gloucester House nursing home for two weeks. It was not till the
middle of June, when I joined Prince Henry during his tour of
Queensland, that I was able to resume my public duties. It was
the first of several tours we were to make in the more isolated
parts of the country, all of which we much enjoyed.

On 23 June I describe a visit to Augustus Downs, one of the
cattle stations on our itinerary. 'All the farm hands were aborigines from the district . . . There was a dear old fellow called
"King Davy". He had it written on a brass plaque hung round his
neck. Before our arrival he had a long white beard which he
shaved off out of respect to Harry. He would not call Harry "The
Duke of Gloucester" but insisted on referring to him as "The
King's Brother". They all seemed thrilled to see us and also the
aeroplane. During the Corroboree which they gave one evening
after dinner they danced and sang a song which was supposed
to represent our arrival and they spread their arms out like the
wings of an aeroplane and made all sorts of strange noises!

'Later that day we flew to a small town called Longreach,

[154]

stopping for ½ an hour "en route" at a very small place called Winton that had an aerodrome. We landed and met all the people on the airfield. There must have been two or three hundred, who had come in from far and near. They sang "God Save the King" as we got out of the aeroplane. It seemed particularly touching somehow in this wide open space without a house in sight.'

In Charleville the only source of water was from hot sulphur springs. We stayed in a little hotel and my sulphur bath miraculously cured the cold I had caught. At Thargaminda, a place of a mere dozen houses, we were in about as remote an area of the inhabitable continent as it was possible to be. There had been no rain for four years but the post was delivered once a fortnight and the people were wonderfully cheerful and contented. In Manteroo, the water from the artesian bore was so hot that it had to be left to cool for a day. It was gratifying for us to know that none of these places had been previously visited by a Governor-General.

At intervals I sent parcels of supplies to my relatives in England. Even at Christmas my presents were functional to a degree, the most successful being sheepskin coats, for one of which I received a characteristically charming letter of thanks from Princess Elizabeth. The most basic foods were still in short supply, and on one occasion I sent Queen Mary a dozen eggs buried for protection and fresh-keeping in a tin of lard. What became of them our correspondence does not relate. Food in Australia was not only plentiful but also good; though meals for official functions, as in most corners of the globe, tended to be unimaginative. Lunches, especially, seemed always to consist of cold ham and turkey, with ices to follow in the form of apples, pears and peaches, that were frozen so hard that they invariably shot off the plate as soon as one applied a spoon or fork. Helpings, which were served already on one's plate like a dog's dinner, were too big to finish, and one felt awful leaving so much good food uneaten when people at home were still half-starved.

By now it was generally known that, because of George VI's decision to visit South Africa with the Queen and Princesses early in 1947, Prince Henry would have to relinquish the

Governor-Generalship in order to preside over affairs of state in England as the King's representative during the Royal Family's absence. Accordingly plans were drawn up for us to embark on a vast farewell tour of cities and towns, villages and stations. Meanwhile we had returned from the parched hinterland to find Canberra under a dusting of snow.

Plans could turn out to be equally confusing and unexpected. An inspection of convalescent homes prompted me to mention on 17 July that 'we motored to the next Home – which we had been told by the Sydney Red Cross, was a Convalescent Home for ex-service *women*. So when we found on arrival a guard of honour of hard-bitten old "Diggers" we were slightly taken aback! Apparently it had ceased to be a Convalescent Home for Service Women in 1943!!'

People were always extremely anxious to see the children so we introduced them as often as possible, usually with refreshing consequences! At one cocktail party, for instance, William was put in charge of Dame Mary Hughes, a rather stout lady. Surveying the company assembled in the drawing room at Canberra, she spied Richard at the far end of the room and said she would like to meet him too. 'Oh yes,' said William manfully, aged three, 'I'll take you to him.' But after much unproductive pushing and shoving on her behalf he declared: 'I'm very sorry, we'll have to go round by the corridor. You're too fat.' On another occasion we all went to plant a tree at the spot where Captain Cook first landed. After shaking hands with the official party and wives on the land-stage William looked rather disappointed and asked: 'But where's Captain Cook?'

Our leave-taking began in Brisbane, from where we made an 8½ hour flight to Darwin in the Northern Territory. We were getting ready for a garden-party on the evening of our first full day, when my maid said: 'I wouldn't have the iced coffee if I were you.' 'Really? Why not?' I asked. 'I've just seen it being made in the washing machine.' There were other discomforts. The sand-flies were so blood-thirsty I had to cover my legs with a towel during lunch, and at a place called Elsie Station crocodiles bathed in what was to become our drinking water; there were disagreeably large spiders in abundance and we had to sleep on a mattress stuffed with two hundred cows' tails.

Elsie Station was the same size as the state of Victoria but belonged to a rather unattractive and generally absentee landlord; so – apart from its enormous size – we could never understand why it was thought desirable for us to go there. However it was, and we were duly met by the owner and his wife – she very unsuitably dressed in black silk. Her replies to my opening questions soon confirmed that she knew almost as little about her property as I did. We met a nice manager, whom we looked forward to seeing again at dinner, but were dismayed to find had not been asked to any meal, apparently because our hosts considered him too much of a social inferior to eat with us.

Next day we were driven to see some tree named after a famous pioneer called Mrs Gunn. When we had taken a photograph and got back into the car for the return journey, the 'digger' who was acting as chauffeur turned to our host and said cheerily: 'Very sorry, sir, I'm afraid I'm bushed!' – lost, in other words. The old man not surprisingly was unable to help, but became so agitated and offensive that I was quite worried for our safety myself. I looked imploringly at the driver and, to my relief and astonishment, he gave me a long and knowing wink. We proceeded to bump off down a track and after a short time – and to the exasperation of the landlord – arrived back at Mrs Gunn's tree. 'Crikey!' exclaimed the driver, without much conviction, 'I must have taken the wrong road. Let's try this one.' And off we bumped again. Needless to say he knew the way backwards and, having got even with his boss, brought us home without further ado. One could well sympathise. It transpired that the landlord had in fact never visited the station before, despite having owned it for several years. Later, when the film 'The Overlanders' appeared, we recognised that they had used Elsie Station as the location.

This rather bizarre experience over, we travelled, indirectly, to Alice Springs, the centre of the continent. Here we opened the town's first hospital and then passed the night in the building, as it was deemed the most suitable accommodation. We also inaugurated the local flying doctor service. In my report to Queen Mary I continued: 'In the afternoon we went to the Races. Very amateur and much more amusing in consequence. People came from hundreds of miles away and all got wildly excited during the races. We went to a dance that night to which all the inhabitants who liked could go. The whole town went so you can imagine the mixture, but it was rather fun and everybody so happy. The floor was asphalt and had a few holes and cracks in it. Not too good for one's best shoes! (Or one's feet the next day!).'

After so much heat and desert South Australia proved a soothing change. Lindsay Park, Angaston, I wrote, 'is a delight-fully comfortable and attractive house . . . the surrounding country is very pretty, undulating, with rich green grass and most lovely old gum trees, scattered about like oak trees in a park.' In Adelaide we stayed with the Governor, Sir Willoughby Norrie, a good friend, who gave us a contrasting glimpse of the future by taking us to Whyalla, a 'remarkable town of about 8,000 which has sprung up in the last few years – The whole place is owned by a company called Broken Hill Proprietary – The same people own iron and steel works and gold mines, etc, all over Australia. Whyalla was situated in flat, waterless, barren country but close to a number of small hills made entirely of rock with a large percentage of iron – Their water supply came from over 280 miles in a pipe from the River Murray (costing £3,000,000).' Our crowded programme at Adelaide included presiding over a garden party for 12,000 guests and attending an official farewell rally given by 7,000 schoolchildren. Willoughby Norrie dismayed me by keeping Prince Henry up late at night by his passion for silly games – like 'polo', in which they all slid about the ballroom on cushions, using spoons for 'sticks' with which to hit a tennis ball. It was in the course of this tour that we also met the famous missionary to the aborigines, Daisy Bates. She was the person responsible for stopping them eating their twins, which they had always been in the habit of doing for some reason.

The farewell programme continued unabated through

September and October, culminating with a memorable visit to Perth and Western Australia, made beautiful at that time of year by a profusion of spring wild flowers. During this trip we travelled along one stretch of railway where we were asked to get out and walk while the train was navigating a rather sharp corner. It appeared that the Prince of Wales had overturned at that point some twenty years before. We returned in the middle of the month, having logged another 5,000 miles, to find William's health again causing concern. He subsequently had his tonsils and adenoids removed in an operation at Government House. 'What a number of doctors you seem to have had for the operation!' commented Queen Mary, before passing on to other topics of interest.

A General Election had confirmed Mr Chifley's Labour Government in power. Mr Chifley was more republican in his convictions than Mr Curtin had been, and indeed refused to meet me on the grounds that he would have nothing to do with Duchesses. I found that the Labour Government could find no seat for me at the Opening of the new Parliament. On one point of etiquette I did notice a change – when we first arrived nobody ever thought of taking off their hats as we drove past, but by the time we left this had changed noticeably.

On 12 January 1947 I broadcast a farewell address. Despite the inconveniences at the outset, the delicacy of the political situation and the ill-health that had dogged us as a family, we much regretted having to leave. The people had given us a wonderful reception wherever we went, and the country and climate had also won our affection. My speech was as follows:

'It is with sadness that I realise the moment has now come for me to say to you women and children of Australia a few words of farewell.

'Up till two months ago we were *still* visiting *new* places and making *new* acquaintances and for many months more we could have gone on doing so; for yours is a large country to cover in two years.

'Amongst the places we have visited have been many that have greatly attracted us, and we would have gladly

[159]

stayed there awhile to enjoy the scenery and visit the homesteads of the people dwelling in those parts.

'But "time and tide wait for no man" and a fleeting visit was all we could ever spare to any one district.

'Add to which – all of you who have ever had small children will, I know, realise there was something else that was calling us and bringing us back home.

'For even if Yarralumla was not really *our* home, it has been so to two small boys too young to remember any other – and a home without a father or mother for too long, is not a good thing.

'Of the many hundreds I have met, so many people have asked me "How do you like Australia?"

'As there was seldom time for me to answer them, maybe they are still wondering.

'I think the shortest and truest answer I could give to that question is: "I like it very much and think it is a fine country which could be finer still."

'It would take more time that I have tonight to give you all my impressions of this country. Covering such vast areas and with such differences of climate and natural surroundings, there must, of course, be a great variety of conditions effecting the lives of the people.

'This we have seen for ourselves, and realised the advantages and disadvantages of different localities.

'I think, on the whole, your lot is fortunate compared with most places in the world at this moment.

'Nature has endowed this country with much that the old country lacks – space and sunshine in particular – and, besides that, I find that your predecessors have brought here the characteristics, the customs and the old traditions of the Mother Country which made her so great through the course of years.

'Please remember these always and never let them die, for they give you the background that would otherwise be missing in a country as young as yours.

'And this brings to mind another question I have so frequently been asked, which is: "Do you find us very different out here from those at home?" My answer has always been: "No, indeed. Why should you be? I find the same familiar names of people and places, the same worries and grumbles, but luckily the same good sense of humour everywhere, as at home. Some people I find more Scotch and some more Irish and some even more English than the English!"

'One thing that I must mention, is, that we have so greatly appreciated the wonderful welcomes given to us everywhere; the eager and expectant faces of the children and their spontaneous and hearty cheers.

'I hope we have fulfilled their expectations, and inspired them to continued loyalty to Crown and Empire, the seeds of which have undoubtedly already been sown by parents and teachers in all districts.

'Time and again I have heard from amongst you kind words such as "Bless you", and "Thank you for coming to see us".

'In case you think I may not have heard I would like to thank you now.

'And to those who were too busy on distant farm and station to come and see us in person, I would like to say that we *did* notice the flags you put on your gateposts to greet us as we motored by, and appreciated that loyal gesture.

'And to you who live in the far-away places, may I say that many a time I looked out on your homes with a bird's eye view from our aeroplane and wondered how you lived and fared; and tried, often in vain, to see a road or track to connect you with somewhere else and realised how hard and often lonely your life must be in such places.

'Now I must say goodbye, and I know that my two sons, too young to speak to you themselves but staying up late to listen to me, would like me to say goodbye to you for them also.

'We shall always remember our time in Australia and send to *all* of you *everywhere* our very best wishes.'

Prince Henry left by aeroplane some weeks ahead of the rest of us, who returned with all the luggage on the *Rangitani*, one of the few New Zealand passenger ships still in service. When we stopped at Pitcairn Island many of the inhabitants came on board with little presents; and at the Panama Canal William was allowed to work the lock. The Governor gave a lunch in our honour and also said he had arranged for a salute to be fired. As we drove along I told William not to be frightened when he heard the guns. A few minutes later there were some 'pops'. 'Are those the guns?' asked William. 'Oh no,' I said. 'Just a motor-bike back-firing.' The Governor who was escorting us, looked rather pained at this and revealed that they had indeed been his salute. We stopped and refuelled again at the Dutch Island of Curaçao in the Caribbean, where we also had lunch with a very charming Dutch Governor and his wife. In the Bazaar I was bitten in the heel by a cat while buying some watches. I had been standing on its tail so perhaps it was hardly surprising. We arrived in London in March. Nearing our journey's end a freak wave hit us and sea water poured in a cascade down the gangway into the dining saloon. Our engines broke down, so we completed the last leg of our voyage assisted by a hastily erected sail.

13

ALMOST THE FIRST THING I did on arriving back in England was to visit the Fens where, owing to melting snow, the banks of the canals, riddled by rat holes, had broken, causing enormous floods. There was mile upon mile of water, with nothing to see but the occasional roof sticking out. We travelled round this pathetic wilderness in an amphibious vehicle called a 'duck'. At Barnwell everything was overgrown – sheep on the lawns, potatoes in the rose gardens; in London we moved back into York House, which had been greatly damaged in the bombing. To put all of this right took a lot of time and effort.

York House being near Marlborough House, I often looked in on Queen Mary for dinner when my husband was out. I would sit talking while she stitched away at a rug she was making, consisting of squares depicting different flowers. She enjoyed working on the flowers but could not be bothered with the background, which was handed over for her lady-in-waiting to finish off. It was eventually bought by Canada in aid of some charity. One of our annual expeditions was always to the British Industries Fair at Olympia. The organisers would always give lunch for the royal party, which was usually attended by the Queen and various government ministers. Queen Mary would lead the procession in a wheel-chair, with everyone else trooping behind. It was quite an undertaking. We generally did two days of it, with her making endless purchases at wholesale prices for bazaars and Christmas presents. She kept a whole room with cupboards full of these. I am sure her activities gave great pleasure to everyone there as well as to ourselves.

Much the same was true of the Antique Dealers Fair. They used to open it for the royal party after dinner, and Queen Mary would again head the cavalcade. She much enjoyed this also; in fact she enjoyed all exhibitions, even when she feared the worst: 'Bertie and E [King George VI and Queen Elizabeth] are coming to London on Monday 23rd for the opening of an Exh. at the V & A Museum, an Exh. of things for *Export*,' she wrote when I was in Australia, 'I hope it will not be too hideous.'

Queen Mary would from time to time come to watch Anne Driver take the music and movement class at York House – a weekly event I had arranged for the boys so that they could meet other children their age. She was an exception to Miss Driver's rule that no onlookers should attend. This was typical of her interest in all matters concerning the family.

In the autumn of 1947 we paid a State visit to Malta to inaugurate a new constitution, arriving back on the eve of the wedding of Princess Elizabeth and Prince Philip. Our William was one of the pages, which gave us much happiness, Princess Elizabeth having been a bridesmaid to us. Christmas was the usual carefree family affair at Sandringham and shortly after, at the beginning of February, we flew out to inaugurate another constitution, this time in Ceylon. On the way we stopped at Habbaniya. The air-force officer looking after us was embarrassed when about to see us off the following morning because he found his trousers had been stolen! Seeing the thief disappearing down the street he let off his pistol, but to no avail.

We also stayed one night in Pakistan. I was much annoyed when somebody burst into our aeroplane shortly after we had touched down and sprayed us all, including my best hat which I had just put on, with insecticide. The partition of India had only just taken place and the visit could not have been made at a more difficult time. Mr Jinnah was Governor-General, an old man with, as it turned out, only a few months to live. I sat next to him at dinner and soon noticed he was in a great state of agitation. Eventually he could contain himself no longer, pouring out all his woes and worries with great indignation. Lord Mountbatten seemed the chief villain in his mind. It was impossible not to feel sorry for him, because he was so clearly upset, but there was nothing I could think of to do about it.

The Ceylonese Parliament was opened in a beautifully decorated hangar, but my most vivid memory of the visit is of a great torch-lit procession of elephants and dancers through the streets of Kandy. Next day I was invited to sit on the knee of the sacred elephant, which had carried the Buddha's tooth in the procession. Such an honour was rarely granted, but the old elephant could not have been more kindly and obliging.

It had been decided that we should avoid Karachi on the flight home but, to our surprise. Mr Jinnah insisted on asking us to dinner again. The second, much more private meal went far better than the first till the coffee arrived, when Mr Jinnah again became angry and excitable about the iniquities of Lord Mountbatten and Britain in general. He harangued my husband on the subject till almost one in the morning. Having run out of breath he stormed out of the room, without saying 'goodnight' to any of us.

In North Africa we stopped to visit some of the recent battlefields. There was not much to remind one of them, though there was some trepidation about land-mines, of which there were apparently still plenty lying around blowing up occasional sheep. We arrived home on 19 February, having flown almost 13,000 miles during the sixteen days of the tour.

In the autumn of that year we made an enjoyable visit to Denmark. This was to attend an Anglo-Danish exhibition and was the first by a member of our royal family since the accession of Frederick VIII – known as 'Ricco' to his family. He had succeeded his father, Christian IX, earlier in the year. We were particularly impressed by the manners and good behaviour of the little Princesses, who curtseyed to everyone including my maid. We were taken by the King and Queen for a delightful trip in the Royal Yacht, visiting many places of interest and stopping for dinner one evening with the Dowager Queen. Finding it too difficult to arrange the seating for dinner we had to draw names for our partner, which resulted in my sitting next to my lady-in-waiting. It was all very informal and somewhat hilarious.

King George's poor health interrupted the long-established

family tradition of Christmas at Sandringham. The King and Queen stayed at Buckingham Palace and we spent Christmas at home. The drawing-room, newly panelled with Boughton oak to a design by Sir Albert Richardson, was much admired when, for the first time, we used it for the estate party. There too we 'saw in' in the New Year; a year that was to be the first of twelve in which we rented Colin Mackenzie's House of Farr in Inverness-shire for the summer holidays.

We had always wanted somewhere to stay in Scotland and Farr seemed just what we needed. It may not have been the most comfortable of houses but it had enough bedrooms for us to squeeze in all the cousins and guests we desired, together with grouse shooting and trout fishing. Situated in beautiful highland countryside, it had innumerable walks and sites for picnics, lovely woods to wander in, a stream running right by the house, and a small island on a loch.

A favourite expedition was to Loch Ness, where we went in hopes of spotting the monster. We took my maid along with us one day. She gazed at the view before her – highland cattle, the Loch, the mountains beyond – and murmured in rapture, 'How lovely, just like a calendar!' I could understand what she meant, though I would not have described it that way myself!

We had a tutor for our sons, whom we all loved dearly. He came each year for the summer holidays – a great help as we knew he would keep a watchful eye on the boys and their friends if my husband and I were away from home. We enjoyed a wonderful feeling of blissful anticipation when the day arrived for us to set off from Barnwell for the North. A vast bus, which we used for luggage in Australia, went ahead driven by Prater, our chauffeur, with guns, fishing rods, our staff and the labrador. We followed in the Rolls, driven by my husband, who hated being driven by anyone else and only let it happen if absolutely necessary. Packed inside would be Mr Robson, the tutor, the two boys and three Australian terriers, and following behind came Amos, who was the valet, Mrs Amos and their little boy. We usually broke our journey with a night at Drumlanrig or with my sister-in-law in Melrose. I think these Scottish holidays were the

[166]

happiest days of all, for which I shall forever be thankful.

My brother Billy and sister-in-law Rachel invariably came to stay with their two youngest children. Among others who came regularly were Princess Alice, Countess of Athlone, and Prince Henry's sister, the Princess Royal. The Princess Royal, in particular, much enjoyed an expedition to visit the shops in Inverness and would spend ages wandering round Woolworths, all on her own, till one or other of us went to collect her.

The tradesmen in Inverness would frequently give parcels of meat, bread, etc to the bus-driver to put on top of the wall as he passed by our gate, and they were always there when someone went to collect them in the evening. The local people were very honest and so apparently were the passers-by. They would not remain there for long nowadays!

The only remotely official event we attended was the local flower show and fête. The Princess Royal usually managed to win the three-legged race with one of the children and she also gave away the prizes at the Flower Show. Mrs Trotter, the redoubtable organiser of the event, donated these. She owned a large garden nearby and the prize-giving ceremony inevitably meant the Princess Royal handing back to her all the prizes – consisting mostly of half-crowns – she had given in the first place!

Princess Alice, for her part, had a habit of going out and picking the most poisonous looking mushrooms, which she would then unsuccessfully try to make us eat. The Princess Royal was likely to return from such forays with her pockets weighed down with stones or shells. These she would subsequently put in bowls filled with water to bring out the colours. One morning William and the chauffeur's little boy persuaded Princess Alice to take them for a walk. On the way back they realised they were going to be late for lunch and accordingly tried to take a short cut, which landed them up against a high deer fence. Looking around, the boys soon found a dry ditch that allowed them to wriggle underneath the wire. They then inveigled Princess Alice into doing the same, one of them pushing and the other pulling. She thought it a great joke.

[167]

Prince Henry would be out most days shooting with neighbours, or often, of course, at Farr itself. He also liked fishing. On one occasion we went over to Beaufort Castle, home of the Lovats, which that summer was let to a rich American lady, Mrs Hammond. Prince Henry fished while we sat around the river bank, but he caught nothing. Mrs Hammond, however, with commendable tact and foresight, had bought a salmon from the fishmonger for just such an emergency, and had already put it in the boot of our car. She also ordered a plateful of roast chicken, sausage and bacon to be given to each of the Australian terriers. This we did not realise was happening till too late and, much to our annoyance, they sicked it all up on the way home.

Prince Henry also liked walks and picnic expeditions. One of the great excitements of the early days at Farr was to go and watch John Cobb testing his speed-boat on Loch Ness in preparation for his attempt to become the fastest man on water. Luckily we were not there the morning he was killed when the boat blew up.

One of the most memorable visits by a celebrity to Farr was paid by Paul Getty, the oil billionaire. He was staying with our friends the Maxwells, and arrived in an enormous car to join us for lunch with 'the guns'. He could hardly have been dressed more inappropriately for a rough day on the hill, wearing an almost white cotton suit and long, pointed black shoes, and was already blue with cold when he arrived. Feeling sorry for him I insisted he wear Prince Henry's stalking cape, which he did with some relief. I told him that his car was too big for the hill road and he would have to come in mine. This also seemed agreeable enough to him, but he winced when it was revealed that I was to be the driver, and did so even more perceptibly when I hit a rock on the roadside that was hidden by a clump of heather. Once out of the car I forgot to warn him that the greenest moss was also the wettest, and he was soaked to the knees before he made the discovery for himself.

At lunch he appeared to have no idea how to sit on the ground and perched himself gingerly on the picnic-basket. Trying to think of something to say to break one particularly heavy silence, my nephew Walter Scott, then a schoolboy, observed: 'My stars say this is a day of financial gains.' One of the guests produced a two bob piece but Mr Getty disregarded the ensuing giggles. He stayed for tea at the house, where he was delighted to discover from his pedometer that he had managed to walk one and a quarter miles in the day. He celebrated by eating a whole ginger cake, remarking that he had never tasted anything half so good. When he left I asked him for the cape, which he was still wearing. Apologetically, but with some reluctance, he handed it over.

One afternoon an expedition which appeared on the map to be enjoyable and by no means difficult, was to cause me a half-hour or more of great anxiety. We had set off that morning for a picnic lunch at one of our favourite lochs. Feeling energetic, the boys and I decided it would be a splendid idea to climb up over the ridge behind us and down the far side. Meanwhile Prince Henry with the Princess Royal chose to drive round and wait for us on the other side at an appointed farm. Our climb looked no distance on the map, but for Richard and me it turned out to be a long and exhausting trek.

We started off at the foot of a small burn tumbling down the mountain side. There was a sheep-track on either side. I elected to take the easy one, winding up a grassy slope; the more adventurous William decided he would climb the steep straight one up through stony rocks. I told him to wait for us at the top, but on arriving there we found no William. Ahead of us lay a long expanse of boggy ground and on our right a long, dark, deep looking tarn with high sheer rocks on its farther side. I half-dragged, half-carried Richard through the squishy moss and peat hags. On reaching the far side there was still no sign of William to be seen. I really felt alarmed and imagined him falling over those steep cliffs into the tarn below. Hot and exhausted, we eventually came to where the hill sloped down to the valley below. Much to my relief there was the road, the farm and the waiting car. Some distance away to the right was a small figure stepping swiftly down the mountain side and almost there. Needless to say it was William, who had found a better, firmer, track on the mountain top, well away from the tarn and the bog we had struggled through on our roundabout way. I felt furiously angry with him for giving me such anguish; then I remembered my mother's anger when my sister and I were nearly drowned at Seascale, and for the first time realised 'why'.

The highlight of the holiday was always the week we spent at Balmoral. Once, however, Richard was in a great state of agitation on the day we left Balmoral to return to Farr. Apparently Princess Anne – then five or six years old – had burst into his room that morning as he was packing, seized his dirk, and saying 'I've always wanted to do this!', had plunged it into the eider-down right to the mattress. I told him he should have explained this to the Queen or the housekeeper, otherwise they would all think he had done it. 'No,' he said resolutely, 'I couldn't tell on her.'

Prince Charles and Princess Anne would visit us at Barnwell from time to time. When bicycling was still a novelty for them, they found it exciting to bicycle through the ford in the village. The stream was about three inches deep and they could make quite a splash. With them would come Nana Lightbody, no doubt delighted to be again with her previous charges and at having an opportunity to meet many old friends.

In the autumn of 1949 I visited the Army of Occupation and various Air Force hospitals in Germany, proceeding to Vienna to pay a call on my Northamptonshire regiment. At that time Vienna was divided between the Allies and the Russians. The airport was in the Russian zone, so I had to travel through the Russian controlled part of the city to reach the British zone. All along the route the Austrians rushed from their houses or waved from windows, blowing kisses and deliberately infuriating the Russians by the warmth of their welcome. Just how furious they were was revealed a day later, when news reached us that our route to a 'Sundowner' at the Officers Mess had been blocked at the last minute by the 'breakdown' of a Russian train on a level-crossing. They had done it on purpose, of course, and thus succeeded in making us take an eight mile detour and arrive late. The Regiment were quartered in barracks built by Hitler, greatly superior to most of ours in England.

[170]

1950 marked the golden jubilee of Nairobi, capital of Kenya, and to mark the occasion we were sent out with a magnificent 'Mace' to confer the status of a 'city' on the town by the grant of a Royal Charter. On the way we stopped in Cairo, so that Prince Henry could present King Farouk with a Field-Marshal's baton, which was the only honour George VI could think of as being suitable. It was not a great success, however, because the King was rather put out to find no uniform went with it. As he was a decidedly strange shape by then, it would have been asking a lot of any tailor to make such a thing without a fitting. Still, he soon swallowed his pride and asked us to a tea of sickeningly sweet sticky cakes. Prince Henry, not having at all a sweet tooth, found this a great ordeal.

Tea finally over, the King asked us if we would like to see his dogs. He appeared to be under the impression that there was nothing Prince Henry would rather do. Prince Henry was fond of his own dogs, it is true, but not particularly interested in other people's; however, we tried to appear enthusiastic and proceeded to follow the King on a tour of some dismal and smelly kennels, where half a dozen dispirited alsatians languished in the heat. In Kenya we began our visit travelling around, staying at Deloraine and meeting many old friends. The day of the Charter ceremony happened to be Prince Henry's fiftieth birthday, and the crowds touched us greatly by bursting into a spontaneous rendering of 'Happy Birthday', which echoed down the street.

William went to boarding-school for the first time in the autumn to Wellesley House, Broadstairs. We were relieved to hear that he had settled down and had enjoyed his journey to Broadstairs, the first he had taken by train since coming to England. Much to the agitation of the master in charge he disappeared at one moment, to be discovered eventually on the luggage rack. Apparently he had done it for a bet! We always went to visit the boys at half-term, for which the headmaster, Mr Boyce, would kindly lend us his house. Richard followed William when the time came and both subsequently passed their common entrance exams into Eton.

Our boys were brought up with as little fuss and formality as we could contrive. As a child William was keen on riding, but Richard could not be bothered to put on breeches and a cap and preferred his bicycle. I used to take them hunting occasionally which I think they enjoyed, certainly it was less worrying for them than it was for me, with William going one way and Richard another. We decided not to buy hunters again and kept one stableman only to look after our two polo pony hacks and the children's ponies. He had been with my husband before we married and remained with us till too old to work any longer. Prince Henry and I would ride round the estate every morning whenever possible, and often the boys would come with us. Prince Henry also took great interest in teaching them to shoot. He was happy in joining them in outdoor occupations – croquet, bonfires, picnics, cricket – leaving me to do most of the indoor entertaining, like reading stories.

Cricket matches were always a tradition of the early days of August. There was an annual fixture with our neighbours, the Wolseley Lewis's under-thirteens, which usually ended up with both teams in the swimming pool. There was also an annual Barnwell-Sandringham estate match, in which Prince Henry liked to play. The XIs consisted of all ages, old and young. There were quite a lot of boys in the vicinity at that time, and with the help of a few of William's or Richard's school friends we usually had little difficulty in mustering sides. With everyone growing at different rates there were, inevitably, some shocks from year to year. One summer the Barnwell policeman's little boy missed a match because he had measles, but next year he was still eligible so we invited him again. A six foot tall youth appeared, who turned out to be him, and proceeded at great speed to bowl out the little boys on the opposing side to the horror and consternation of their parents. We were very embarrassed and frantically signalled to William to take him off, but he paid not the slightest attention. Luckily there were no casualties.

The children's early school years were comparatively quiet ones for us. We both enjoyed country life, and at Barnwell found plenty to occupy us in those moments when we were free of public obligations. I always wrote my own speeches but Prince

Henry seldom did, and disliked delivering them just as much. He was the sort of person whom it was difficult to get started in time. He would never be ready – fussing over details, looking for papers and remembering last minute instructions for this and that. Even visiting the boys at Eton we would sometimes arrive an hour late. I would be in agonies on the journey, thinking of them waiting forlornly, wondering what had become of us. No doubt they knew perfectly well.

Some events were a particular strain for Prince Henry and in consequence for me also: perhaps most of all the Trooping the Colour, with an uncomfortable uniform and a horse, which probably hated the elaborate harness and trappings. Many occasions such as agricultural shows we used to attend together. Prince Henry particularly enjoyed race meetings which held personal memories for him, Aldershot races and the Grand Military Cup, which is now run at Sandown. After he died I presented a trophy in his memory to be raced for at Sandown at the Grand Military meeting.

At Barnwell, however, he was busy and contented. There was plenty to do. When we bought the Manor, most of the land was farmed by tenants but, because of the anticipated difficulty of dealing with their demands while we were in Australia, we sold most of the estate. Rather to our surprise, it fetched a larger sum than we had originally paid for the entire property. On our return we started to build a dairy and farm buildings, but the land we had retained was not large enough to be economical so, with the proceeds of the sale of the tenanted farms, we began to buy back untenanted land near Barnwell as it came up for sale and thus increased our holding to an estate today of over 5,000 acres. The farm was run in a somewhat casual way by present standards, and probably never paid, but this was as much a reflection of the times as anything.

Prince Henry always improved and modernised as best he could; but the organisation was less professional in those days than it is now. We shared a land agent with Boughton and only retained a clerk at Barnwell to handle the accounts. Today the farm is run as a business. A firm audits the accounts, we have a resident manager and even an expert, who visits once a month to advise Richard on matters of overall policy. In the early days we used to employ a number of nice old men who continued to do the odds and ends of lighter work till the day they died. That sort of person does not appear to exist any longer.

While Prince Henry concentrated on the farm, I kept an eye on the garden. He worked there too from time to time, especially cutting down bushes, but only if I was there with him. On his own it bored him. We enjoyed collecting antiques for the house and doing the rounds of the London shops in search of his favourite *netsuke*, miniature elephants, sporting prints, pictures and books. His favourite bookseller never much appreciated my coming, as I would question some of his prices, whereas Prince Henry paid whatever was suggested without a murmur. 'Oh goodness!' I would say, 'we can't afford that, we really can't!' The bookseller would give me a withering look; and then next time he might say casually, 'Oh, by the way, I've found a rather less expensive copy of that book we were looking at on your last visit' – and produce what was probably exactly the same volume for our inspection.

The King's death in 1952 at such a relatively early age was a shock and sadness to us all; and a great blow to Prince Henry, who was devoted to his brother and relied greatly on his good advice. Having had illnesses and difficulties of his own, George VI was an understanding and kind-hearted brother-in-law. It was typical of him, who did not like writing, to send me a long and comforting letter the moment Prince Henry was despatched abroad at the beginning of the war.

A year later we were again filled with sadness, this time for the death of Queen Mary. The Duke of Windsor stayed with us at York House for the funeral, and there was one evening when the Princess Royal came to dinner and the sister and two brothers sat up till the early hours of the morning discussing old friends and past times. It was particularly moving listening to the Duke, because he was obviously so pleased to be talking with his own family again. The conversation was so personal to the three of them, that I almost felt I should not have been present.

Our spirits were soon to be lifted again, however, by the Coronation. We must have been up by five o'clock that morning, getting the boys dressed in their new kilts and coats and my husband and I in our robes and orders. It was a memorable occasion for us all, though the long drive after the ceremony – mostly in the pouring rain – was rather tedious for the boys. We drove in the same carriage as the Princess Royal, who kept them amused with funny stories of past events. My husband was riding in the procession. The enthusiasm of the vast crowds seemed unaffected by the rain and the discomfort for many of having slept out on the pavement the night before and breakfasted there.

In August, 1957, Prince Henry, on behalf of the Queen, presided over the independence celebrations of Malaya. William was now fifteen and we took him with us so that he might gain experience. The evening before we left Farr was particularly beautiful and we all went for a stroll on the moors. I was going to visit my Scottish regiment, the King's Own Scottish Borderers, during the forthcoming tour and Rachel Scott suggested I take them a bundle of heather as a reminder of home. Prince Henry was horrified at the idea, protesting that we had more than enough luggage to cart around already, but we paid no attention and soon collected enough to fill a large polythene bag. When William and I later visited the regiment in the Malayan jungle, our bundle proved sufficient to give every soldier a sprig for his bonnet. They were thrilled – and for the first time heather bloomed in the jungle.

On our way out we stopped to refuel in Cyprus and went to have a drink with our friends the Hardings. The war between the Greeks and Turks on the island was at its height so we were heavily guarded. A message came to say that some part in our aeroplane had to be replaced and it would take some hours to do – so we stayed on for dinner, after which most of the party wandered out into the cool of the garden. Lady Harding and I remained indoors talking about the horrors of the war, and she told me about the unexploded bomb they had found under the General's bed and on top of which he had slept soundly all night.

Stepping outside to join the rest of the party we were startled to see a large black object hurtling towards us across the lawn; but after an anxious few seconds we realised it was only a crocquet ball, apparently let loose by William from behind some bushes.

In Malaya it was hot and wet, but everything went more or less to plan. Prince Henry woke one morning at two and said furiously: 'Who's having a bath at this hour of the night?' but actually it was the noise of the rain clattering on a tin roof outside. The monsoon had arrived. The KOSB's were stationed in the south of the country, miles from anywhere. I travelled in a two-seater aeroplane, William in another, and the lady-in-waiting in the third. When we arrived at the landing-strip we were received by a guard of honour of headhunters attached to the Regiment, who were very surprised to find the Colonel-in-Chief was a small female in a silk frock rather than a towering officer with bristling moustache and feathers flying from his hat. On our way to the camp I asked the CO, Colonel McConnell, why a village we had passed through showed no sign of celebrating their new-found independence. 'Oh, they won't hear about that for at least three years!' he replied.

Travelling back to England we stopped briefly in Ceylon, where William was given a very special tortoise. It was duly stowed alongside some equally special orchids, with which we had been presented in Malaya, and by the time we reached Kinloss it had eaten the lot. It suffered no ill effect – on the contrary, the animal can still be seen at London Zoo. The Foreign Office also had us call on the ruler of Bahrein. He invited us to share some coffee and, during a rather stilted conversation, asked me what it was like in our aeroplane. I told him we had beds and that it was fitted out in the height of comfort. With that his eyes lit up and he asked if he could come and see it. The whole party, accordingly, trooped back, followed by a swarm of flies, through the heat to the York. The Arabs were so impressed that they wanted to order one then and there. Then they left, leaving all the flies behind them. The York was the one we had in the Governor-General's flight, when in Australia, lent to us again for this occasion.

14

IN 1958 AND 1959 we made extensive tours of Africa. The first, in November, began with a visit to the Emperor Haile Selassie of Ethiopia. We were delayed by a fog, which puzzled the Ethiopians very much, not knowing what a fog was! Prince Henry inspected a Guard of Honour on our arrival at the palace. He sensed something large and hot sniffing at his heels as he walked along and when he turned at the end of the row discovered that he was being followed by a lion. Luckily it was a well-fed pet of the Emperor's. I was taken to see the royal grandchildren at their lessons, dear little girls and boys being instructed by an Englishman and his wife. Alas, many of them must now be murdered or languishing in prison. Our maid and valet set off as soon as they could to do some shopping in the bazaar. They met two corpses hanging from gibbets, which rather put them off, and they returned hurriedly.

The Emperor led an austere life, and was much worshipped by the Court. Everyone fell to his knees whenever he entered the room. I found him charming, kindly and interesting. The only trouble was that he always spoke in French, at which I was not very good. The Empress was equally charming – a large, shy woman. Our first evening was marked by a state banquet. While we were dressing for dinner, the Prime Minister arrived at our bedroom door with an Order for me from the Emperor – the Badge and Star of the Queen of Sheba – and said he must pin it on me personally. As I was only half-dressed this was out of the question; however he insisted till my maid, after a heated argument, somehow chivvied him into handing it over in the passage. He retired disgruntled. The banquet proved a magnificent spectacle, with ninety-nine guests eating off a service of silver gilt from Aspreys – the food presented by footmen dressed in green jackets, maroon velvet breeches and white stockings. Apart from this one grand dinner and the elaborate deference shown to the Emperor, court life was remarkably simple.

We were taken to visit a hospital that had a new wing built in memory of the Emperor's daughter, a Princess who had died when quite young. She had trained as a nurse in England. A patient of special interest had been singled out for me to meet, but when we arrived at his room he was nowhere to be seen. Our hosts were embarrassed and worried. Later we were told that the occupant, on hearing us approach, had been so seized with fear that he had hidden in the cupboard. At another hospital in Gondar we found they had an armed guard at the end of each ward to protect the patients from their enemies, who were apt to rush in and murder them.

When we left we exchanged gifts and photographs in the traditional way. The youngest son of the Emperor was surprised to receive something for himself and vanished, only to reappear a moment later with two little parcels for William and Richard done up in Christmas wrapping paper. They turned out to be ash-trays with the imperial cipher on them, suspiciously like the ones on our bedside tables. We only hoped the Emperor did not think *we* had pinched them!

After Ethiopia we went to Somaliland. We had wanted to go there first, but apparently that would have upset Haile Selassie because it would have looked as if Britain thought Somaliland more important than Ethiopia. Here too I visited a hospital. There was a sick-looking old lady who caught my attention, and I asked them what was wrong with her. 'She's been very badly bitten by one of her neighbours,' they said. The human bite, so it transpired, is especially poisonous.

Our brief stay was spoilt for me by a sandgrouse shoot that was arranged for the benefit of Prince Henry. We were driven before dawn to some distant water-holes, to which thousands of sand-grouse flocked at first light from the surrounding desert. They were very easy to shoot, since in spite of being driven away again and again by the guns their need to drink over-rode their fear of death and back they would come relentlessly. It was horrible. Afterwards, as a most unwelcome reminder, our hosts gave us a sackful of the dead birds to take back to England. This proved an awkward present. They filled up the fridge and then, when we got home, no one wanted to eat them. In the end we dumped them on a nearby hospital, but I doubt if anyone could be bothered to pluck them.

During our visit we handed out the customary selection of walking sticks, watches and framed and autographed photographs of ourselves, and received, among other things, two baby cheetahs – small enough to fit into a shoe-bag – and a polo pony. These unexpected gifts also proved rather a burden. We were bound for Aden, where we were to end our tour, and the pony had to follow by boat because it could not be fitted into our aeroplane. In Aden they promised to forward the animal to England when a suitable ship could be found, but on arrival it was discovered to be suffering from some dreadful bone disease so that was the end of that.

The cheetah cubs, a male and female, we took with us. They were adorable to look at but scratched viciously and had to be fed every four hours on raw meat. When we arrived in Aden they were temporarily taken off our hands by Miss Luce, the Governor's daughter, who proved a tireless keeper. The male did not seem to want to move; but the female rushed everywhere. Then came the difficult decision of how to get them back to England without their dying of cold. We packed them as best we could in rolls of cotton-wool, but they died nonetheless, to the great disappointment of the Zoo who were longing to have them. An autopsy revealed that the male had various broken bones. The mother had presumably been shot for her skin, and the cub's bones broken when it was grabbed by the trappers. It was sad; they were such sweet little things.

A memory of Somaliland – repeated in other countries on our

many travels over the years – was of an old chief telling Prince Henry how sad he was at the prospect of independence, because he and others of his age could well remember the days before British rule and how terrible they had been. But it was no use; their sons would not listen, saying they knew just as well as the British how to run their country. I expect by now many of them would agree with the old man.

The following May we returned to Africa, this time on a state visit to Nigeria and the North Cameroons. We started at Kano in the north. The Emir was a splendid old man who shuffled about in a wonderful pair of shoes, like bedroom slippers sprouting ostrich feathers all around. While Prince Henry visited some students, the Emir took me to meet his wives and children, male visitors not being allowed. The palace buildings were quite large but made entirely of mud. I was received in a grand room with a vaulted ceiling and walls encrusted with unlikely objects. A large area was lined with recurring cardboard squares of little tin cake moulds, the glitter of which obviously appealed to the inhabitants; and there were shelves of oddities, including five tin horses in the form of pogo sticks meant for small children to jump up and down on. The walls of one of the Emir's own most prized rooms were embedded with china plates, and a fridge stood in the middle of his bedroom.

He proudly introduced me to a number of his children. Luckily I had brought enough Edinburgh rock to give them each a little box. I was then conducted behind the scenes on an inspection of the living-quarters, where some of his smaller children were terrified and rushed away screaming at the sight of me. I could only suppose they had never seen a white face before. Later, visiting a hospital in another district, I was no less surprised to find that little black babies are pink at birth. Apart from the toddlers, everyone was friendly and pleased to see me.

At a dinner given for us at Government House, to which various Nigerian dignitaries came, one emir proudly showed me his most treasured possession, a button from the waistcoat of the nineteenth-century Scottish explorer, Mungo Park, worn as a ring. At the end of the meal cigars in little aluminium tubes were offered to the gentlemen, most of whom, being Mohammedan, were forbidden to smoke. An emir next to me nevertheless took one of these, whereupon another opposite us said rather sharply across the narrow table: 'You don't smoke, do you?' To this my Mohammedan neighbour replied: 'Oh no, I only want the tube'. No doubt he smoked it later in secret.

Dinner parties throughout the tour tended to be timeless affairs. On one occasion, however, the fault was inadvertently ours. When travelling in places like Africa I always made a point of taking my own supply of Malvern Water to drink. At this particular lunch we waited so long that in the end I could not resist asking the ADC to find out the cause of the delay. He returned with the news that Miss Malvern Waters had still not arrived! Apparently some memorandum of my need for 'Malvern Water' had found its way on to the guest list.

A magnificent durbar was held in our honour before we left the Northern Region. In the great parade one of the emirs appeared on an elephant. This annoyed his fellow dignitaries very much, since none of them had come on anything taller than a camel. Camels seemed to serve many purposes. When Prince Henry opened the library of one school he asked the headmaster whether he could give the pupils a holiday to commemorate his visit. 'Oh no!' exclaimed the headmaster. 'A holiday is the worst punishment of all because they're mad keen to come to school and places are very scarce. Could you give them a feast?' For this we had to supply a camel, which apparently was considered a great delicacy!

During the tour we visited the North Cameroons. This neighbouring state formerly belonged to Germany, which explained why the High Commissioner's lodge, where we stayed half-way up Mount Cameroon, was built like a German *schloss*. We drove from sea level where it was very hot, put on cardigans as we climbed and finally donned overcoats for the last freezing ascent to the *schloss*. Mount Cameroon was a live volcano, still smoking from a recent eruption. Half-way up, its atmosphere was as damp as it was cold, thirty feet of rain falling in an average year as opposed to thirty inches in England. We were advised not to leave our shoes uncovered overnight as they would be enveloped in mildew by the morning.

I longed for a walk, which people in this sort of country seldom seemed to take, so rather unwillingly Mrs Field, the Commissioner's wife, said she would accompany me. First we passed the local prison, which worried Mrs Field because she thought somebody might escape at that instant (I was later told that this was unlikely as everybody loved being there because the food was so good); and then, in the middle of a charming little wood, we were both equally alarmed by a sudden rumbling under our feet. 'Goodness,' I said, 'I hope there isn't going to be another eruption!' With that we hurried home, only to discover that the rumblings had been the local water supply being turned on.

Back in England we resumed the official round. Something Prince Henry particularly enjoyed was to give away prizes at Wellington College every year. He always made a point of going by helicopter, because it gave the boys such pleasure to see their parents' hats blown off. In the course of a year there would inevitably be numerous dinners to attend. One never knew whom one would be sitting next to, but there was always some subject of mutual interest if one could only discover it. Winston Churchill when placed next to me knew that he would never be short of champagne. I do not drink, but I would let my glass be filled so that Winston could have the benefit of it when he had finished his.

Once, at the Guildhall, I had to sit next to General de Gaulle. First he complimented me on the beauty of my daughter and then asked how I had enjoyed my recent visit to the chateaux of the Loire. The banquet was being given by Sir Edmund and Lady Stockdale, who were the Lord and Lady Mayoress of the time, and I realised from these remarks that the General was under the impression that I was his hostess. Since I was sitting on his right this was a perfectly reasonable assumption; accordingly, while he was talking to somebody else, I quickly pushed my name card his way. This did not work, however, because he was very short-sighted, so not wishing to embarrass him, I remained Lady Stockdale for the rest of the evening!

Our twelve year lease on the House of Farr was coming close to its end. When it had run out we took Tulchan, a large and comfortable house in Morayshire, for the last few summers before my husband's health deteriorated. Here again there was grouse shooting and salmon fishing on the Spey, but we did not like it as much as Farr, which we had all come to love so dearly. To get on to the heather you had to make your way through a thick pine wood for about an hour and a half before you reached it, and by then it was usually time to come home; and a busy main road near the house meant we were perpetually worrying for the safety of the dogs. Fortunately there was an attractive path leading down to the river, which was perfect for my husband's evening walk.

In May 1961, I accompanied Prince Henry, who was President of the Commonwealth Graves Commission, on a tour of military cemeteries in Greece and Turkey. The Queen happened to be on a state visit to Italy ending in Venice aboard the Royal Yacht *Britannia* and when she flew home she kindly lent us the yacht for our tour. This was especially nice for me as my brother-in-law, Peter Dawnay, happened to be Captain. Under normal circumstances he would not have been allowed to have his wife aboard, but I was able to take Angela as my lady-in-waiting. John Profumo, then Minister of War, was also in our party, adding to the enjoyment of all. *Britannia* is very comfortable, with a large dining-room and drawing-room and spacious cabins. It is designed to be quickly convertible into a hospital ship in time of war.

While stopping the night at Canakkale, the Russian whaling fleet came along to spy on us. We were at anchor when our stewards came to warn us of their approach. Abandoning our tea we rushed on deck, to see nine ships bearing down on us. A little Turkish gun-boat acting as our escort and 'on the alert', went round and round, bravely trying to keep them at a distance. Even so they came perilously close. The Russians were all up on deck to have a good look, and I waved at them as they passed. Not one of them moved till, on about the fifth ship, a solitary figure waved in acknowledgement, only to be immediately removed by two of his colleagues. I felt awful about getting him into trouble, and stopped being friendly forthwith. A Turkish admiral later told me that this Russian fleet, suspecting something unusual was going on, had wasted two days sailing back to see what it could be. During the night, under cover of darkness, they turned to resume their outward voyage.

While my husband was visiting graves I made a short visit to Troy. There were several 'roadblocks' to pass on the way and many soldiers around who looked at us suspiciously. Some of the cemeteries in Macedonia were in remote country near the Bulgarian border, the villages where the gardeners lived were primitive with hovel-like homes, no sanitation and only animal dung for winter fuel. In one house I was horrified to see a lusty three month old baby tightly bound from head to toe in 'swaddling clothes', nothing visible but its face, purple with exasperation. Dogs had great spikes on their collars, apparently as a protection against wolves. At Istanbul the Florence Nightingale hospital had a cage where rabies cases were locked up. It was all rather backward, but the people responsible for the cemeteries were friendly and the graves beautifully tended.

It was amusing, too, to see how well the Australian and New Zealand generals accompanying us on this tour got on with the Turkish Generals, once their bitter enemies at Gallipoli. Each was fascinated to find out why the other had done this and that all those years before. We went one morning to visit one of the few remaining wooden houses on the Bosphorus. It could only be reached by boat, with the entrance at the top of some steps leading straight out of the water. We have heard since that it has been burnt to the ground and the delightful old Turkish gentleman who owned it is possibly no longer alive.

Within a few months we were once more called upon to go abroad, this time to Malta and Kenya. It was February and we arrived at Luqa to find the children thrilled by the first snowfall experienced in Malta within many people's memory. The houses, needless to say, were quite unsuited to such weather,

Cousins in the snow at Sandringham:
(*left to right*) Princess Anne, William, Richard,
Prince Charles, Nanny Lightbody, 1952.

Silver Wedding photograph, 6 November 1960.

My eightieth birthday Christmas card with the grandchildren
at Barnwell: *(left to right)* Rose, Alexander and Davina.

Wearing the Blesma rose –
the rose of the British Limbless ex-Servicemen's Association.

having no heating and windows that refused to shut tightly, so for the one night we were there we all froze. The following day, when Prince Henry presented colours to the Air Force, there was such a gale blowing that the ceremony was moved indoors to the shelter of a hangar. This was not a success. The wind caused the doors to rattle so noisily that it was impossible to catch more than a few words of the address. When we left that night we had to wade out to our aeroplane.

Kenya proved as much of a restorative as ever. At Eldoret Agricultural Show, three regiments – the Scots Guards, Gordon Highlanders and Enniskillen Fusilliers – beat a retreat. Prince Henry, who was Colonel-in-Chief of all three regiments, was photographed with the three pipe majors. The fact that this meeting took place in such distant surroundings, practically on the equator, made it particularly moving. In 1981 when visiting Northern Ireland to present colours to the territorial battalion of what used to be the Enniskillens (now Irish Rangers) at Bally-mena, I mentioned that day at Eldoret in my speech, as a result of which one or two men came forward to tell me they too had been present that day.

Almost exactly a year after our return from Kenya we paid a visit to Jordan at the invitation of King Hussein, to visit St John's Opthalmic Hospital in Jerusalem. Here again it was snowing unseasonally when we arrived. We stayed in a guest-house, carefully guarded by Arab legionnaires. Security was so great that one of these men even stood permanent guard in the 'loo', which was apparently a favourite place for assassins to lie in wait. Whenever one wished to enter one had to wait for the sentry to remove himself. I asked my maid if she thought these men would be of any use if anything really did happen. 'I'm sure they've no idea even which side they're on,' she reassured me.

As usual, before a foreign visit, our office had found out about the customs of the place and had been advised that, in the matter of ladies' evening wear, short black dresses, preferably with long sleeves and high necks, would be correct. Luckily I mentioned this to the Princess Muna at a small reception the King gave for us at his private house before the state banquet. She said that *she* was going to wear her wedding-dress. I and my lady-in-waiting looked at each other in dismay, and as soon as we could, hurried home and unpacked the evening gowns we had taken to wear later at a dance in Cyprus. When we arrived for dinner there was Princess Muna in what had been her wedding dress, sleeveless and with a low neck!

The following evening the King and the Princess were our guests for dinner at the British Embassy. There had been rumours of a 'coup' and when they were late in arriving we began to worry for their safety. When they finally appeared there was a further delay while places at the table were rearranged. The King had been assigned a seat with his back to the window, which would have made him a possible target for assassins, so Prince Henry and Princess Muna were put there instead. The meal began almost in silence and then the Jordanians burst into conversation among themselves in their own language, leaving us guests to look on. After dinner the King showed us some films he had made. Next morning the Jordanian General who was looking after us apologised for what had happened. He explained that being in the British Embassy provided them with their only chance to speak their minds, without fear of being overheard by their enemies.

The Foreign Office had instructed us to visit Cyprus on our way home in order to show the Government's support for President Makarios, who had recently returned from exile in the Seychelles. Relations between the Turkish and Greek Cypriots were still strained, a fact demonstrated for us on our arrival when the President rudely failed to introduce the leader of the island's Turkish community. Our private secretary was at pains to point out how affable the Foreign Office wanted us to be – which we were – and the President was equally friendly. He said he had enjoyed his exile. He was a charming man to meet and converse with.

At Barnwell that June we gave a dance to celebrate William's coming of age. We hired a marquee to serve as a ballroom, the dance floor laid over my carefully planted paving, but the plants somehow survived. The old ruined castle was floodlit and pipers played, and everyone who watched outside was frozen. The Queen brought her train to Barnwell Station and very helpfully put up a number of guests in it for the night. Unfortunately crowds gathered to watch her pass a local level-crossing, causing an unprecedented traffic jam which delayed many of the cars bound for the dance.

The dance served as a climax to William's final year at Cambridge. He had enjoyed his three years at the University, but came down feeling unsatisfied academically. He had read history for want of any other ideas and now he decided to extend his formal education with a year at Stanford University in California, studying the more practical subjects of Economics, Business and Political Science. Richard in turn went to Cambridge. ''Ow d'you find Cambridge?' asked a pressman when he arrived. 'Look it up on a map,' replied Richard. Richard had no more idea of what to read than William, but William, fresh from his own experience, impressed on him the importance of doing a subject he would enjoy and bcause Richard had always been good at making models, suggested architecture. This proved such a success that I am sure that had Richard not succeeded to the title he would, in due course, have become well known in his own right as an architect.

In early 1965 plans were being made for a five week tour of Australia. This included visits to four states. The main event and reason for the tour was the fiftieth anniversary of Anzac Day. A March Past was to be held in front of the War Memorial in Canberra, with Prince Henry taking the salute as the Queen's representative. There was also a new university building to be opened in Melbourne, a bridge in Tasmania (later to be knocked down by a passing ship), the Agricultural Show in Sydney and several days to be spent touring the Snowy Mountains hydro-electric installations.

We were in the midst of preparations for this undertaking when we travelled to London early that year for Churchill's funeral. It was on the drive back to Barnwell that same day that we suffered the car crash from which Prince Henry never seemed fully to recover. We had made an early start that morning, and no doubt Prince Henry was too tired to drive on the return journey. He had recently been told by the doctors to give up driving, but had refused to take their advice and I had not had the heart to argue with him. He had always been an expert driver and by this time, when long walks and shooting were no longer possible for him, it was about the only pleasure left to him.

I always sat beside him ready to grab the wheel or put my foot on the brake if he fell asleep and lost control, but on this occasion I must have dozed off myself, as I have no recollection of what happened. It must have been an awful moment for Prater in the back of the car, seeing everything but unable to do anything about it. Fortunately there was a coach with a Royal Air Force band and a detachment of St John's Ambulance from Mansfield Colliery following closely behind, and they helped us as much as they could. Apparently the Rolls swerved off the road over a ditch and hedge and then, after somersaulting three times, ended upside down in a field of cabbages. Prince Henry had luckily been thrown through the open door into nettles and brambles as the car went over the ditch and was virtually unscathed. As it turned over for the third time the door beside me opened and out I fell, with the car miraculously just missing me.

I have no recollection of these happenings up to the moment I started to regain consciousness and felt the gentle hands of the two miners supporting my body and replacing, as best they could, the end of my nose, while murmuring words of comfort and reassurance. I am sure no one could have done better than they in saving my life and preventing me suffocating from the blood pouring down my throat from my nose. I could not think what was happening or where I could be. The first thing that came to mind was the Queen, in black and carrying a baby. Then other things slowly returned: the funeral service, and the lunch afterwards at Buckingham Palace for the many V.I.P.s. It was after this lunch that Prince Edward had been brought in to be shown to the guests. I suppose I must have been thinking of this when the crash knocked me out.

An ambulance arrived and took us off to Bedford Hospital. Being a Saturday evening most of the doctors had gone off duty and I was left to the attention of a young Cypriot doctor in the casualty ward, who put fifty-seven stitches into my face. He also found I had broken an arm, which he set and put in plaster. Experts, when consulted later, said the injuries could not have been treated better.

I spent the next week or two in the private patients' quarters of the hospital, where my family, including Princess Marina, came to visit me. For the first night I thought I was blind. The nurse realised my anxiety and explained that I could not open my eyelids owing to the bruising. It was a great relief when I was able to open them and found my eyes were none the worse. I was greatly touched by the numbers of cards, letters and flowers that came pouring in – particularly by those with messages of 'get well quickly' scribbled on the outside. They must have been added by the postman or the porters at the station. Apart from the cuts and bits of bone removed from my face, I had a broken arm, a broken nose and a cracked knee. Nevertheless I had sufficiently recovered in five weeks to accompany Prince Henry to Australia, where we arrived only one week later than had been originally planned.

On the day of the great parade at the Australian War Memorial in Canberra, everybody had already left for the ceremony when Prince Henry, who was sitting waiting for Amos to pull his boots on, suddenly said 'I can't get up.' I opened a window, hoping he just felt faint from the heat, and somehow Amos and I managed to support him downstairs. We went round to the car by the garden door rather than through the house, so as to get some fresh air and avoid the staff who were lining the passage. I was most worried but clearly we had to carry on and hope for the best.

Once in the car the chauffeur had to drive very fast to make up time, and this I think helped. At one point we swerved violently to avoid a woman with a pram, which made Prince Henry so angry he quite recovered. I suppose he was in a daze after what must have been a mild stroke, and his sudden irritation with the chauffeur snapped him out of it. I was still anxious about him when we arrived, because looking down a lot of steps always made him dizzy and this was the position he was going to have to maintain for the endless March Past. I warned the Governor-General Lord De L'Isle to keep a watchful eye on him. Fortunately, all went to plan and there was no further mishap.

I often wonder how I managed to compete in those five weeks, with my arm in plaster from shoulder to wrist and a somewhat wobbly knee. People seemed to enjoy helping me along, cutting up my food for me etc. Unfortunately, as a result of my exertions I suffered later that spring from delayed concussion, which worried me not a little till a doctor explained to me what was wrong with me.

Apart from a visit the following year to Malaysia, Singapore and Borneo, when Prince Henry's health was even more precarious, this was the last official visit abroad that we were to conduct together.

In the summer of 1965 William was posted as Third Secretary on the staff of the High Commission in Lagos. During his appointment I went out to see him. He had planned to take me on a tour of favourite spots in his sports car, but unfortunately, just as we were about to set off, civil war broke out again. Instead of having leave, William found himself extra busy at the office. The event could not have happened more dramatically; even the High Commissioner's wife only discovered about it when she went to the airport to meet her children coming out for the holidays and saw soldiers hustling people off at gunpoint in all directions. She grabbed the children and hurried home with the news.

The Americans sent a ship to take away their people, which set the British business community grumbling that nobody was looking after them. The High Commissioner, Sir Francis Cumming-Bruce, thought it would be a good idea in these circumstances to give a garden-party in my honour so as to show that even I had not been taken home. The only sign of change I noticed was the sudden absence of my Nigerian security officer. He had been a dreadful bore, always squeezing himself in wherever I went and quite unnecessarily over-attentive, but as soon as the emergency was declared he vanished. The day I left, he rushed up with hand outstretched, as ingratiating and self-important as ever, no doubt hoping for a large tip – but I paid no attention.

Early in the New Year we made the second of three visits to Runaway Bay in Jamaica. We had to change planes at Kennedy Airport, and the Duke of Windsor took advantage of this interlude to come out from New York to see us. In spite of all that had happened, the brothers were very good friends and really pleased to meet each other. This was to be the last time they did so.

Richard and his friends decided to give a dance in Cambridge at the end of 'May Week' that year, but they applied too late to get a suitable room, so Richard asked if they could hold it in the lovely old barn in the stable-yard at Barnwell. I agreed, on condition that the house itself was roped off so that Prince Henry should not be disturbed. There was an open-air film on the castle wall and bands played in three different places.

At about eleven p.m. my lady-in-waiting and I took a stroll to see what was going on. There were some odd noises coming from the swimming-pool, so we investigated and found the only person there was one of the young rock musicians, playing some instrument. 'Oh dear, has it gone wrong?' I asked, hoping to comfort him. At this he looked indignant and replied: 'Nothing's gone wrong. It's meant to be like that!' During our tour we also came across a young girl dressed like a pre-war debutante, in a beautiful ball gown with long white gloves and pearls. Her mother had obviously assumed it would be a royal occasion and had made her daughter dress accordingly. I felt very sorry for the poor girl because, of course, it could not have been a more informal party. Straw bales served as tables and chairs, and most people appeared to be dressed in a motley collection of their grandparents' clothes, ancient uniforms being very popular at that time.

Princess Anne came to stay with us for the occasion. I think it was her first party away from home and I doubt if she has been to another in the least like it! At about 4 a.m., just as the sun was getting up, I woke to a sound of cuckoos. It was as if every cuckoo in Northamptonshire had gathered to try to drown the noise of the band that was still pounding away in the distance. Looking out of my window I saw several Arabs floating around in white, playing croquet, which completed the strangeness of the moment. Some of the guests parked themselves in tents and caravans in a field beyond the stables, and for the next month or so when weeding the garden, I would find glasses and beer cans among the shrubs and plants.

By the end of 1968 further strokes had made Prince Henry a complete invalid. I would talk to him, hoping he could hear and understand, or show him photographs of things that I thought might interest him. I also read him letters, though I was never quite sure how much he took in. The great thing was to give him the comfort of knowing someone was there; accordingly we always ensured that someone was sitting with him – if not the nurse, then myself or Mrs Holland, my lady-in-waiting, or Lady Seton, my secretary at Barnwell; and, of course, Amos and Prater. I used to ask his old friends to stay as well, so that he could at least see they were still about. Another person who used to come and sit with him was Miss Saxby, the retired matron of King Edward VII's Hospital. She was a great admirer of Prince Henry from the days when he had been her President at King Edward's. Every day, weather permitting, he would be driven on a tour of the farms in a Minimoke fitted with a special comfortable seat, and this was now his greatest pleasure. He would be accompanied by me and all the dogs if I was available, otherwise by Sister Anne, his nurse.

A curious thing once happened. The parrot William had brought back from Nigeria suddenly jumped off her cage on to the floor and looked as if she might be eaten up by 'Holly', one of the labradors, who advanced upon her. To my astonishment Prince Henry, who was unable to speak, shouted the dog's name. I asked his doctor how this could happen? He said it was because the fright side of the brain is different from the speech side.

I had to carry out some of Prince Henry's public commit-ments, and as I never liked to leave him for long this meant much travelling back and forth from Barnwell. William helpfully resigned from the Foreign Service; he was needed to run the estate and also thought it was time he took up some of his father's official responsibilities. Up till then it had not been easy for him to decide what best to do. As parents, we could never quite make out whether our children were supposed to lead royal lives at the command of the Queen or were free to follow professional careers of their choice. Somehow it became clear that William would inherit Prince Henry's duties with the title, and that Richard could do whatever he liked – which was why he became an architect. As it turned out Richard's architectural experience – had to abandon a successful practice when he inherited the Dukedom – has proved very useful in the exercise of his public duties.

William returned in 1970. He had been abroad so long – in America, Africa and finally Japan – and his leaves had been so short, that I felt I had hardly known him as a grown-up man. The sad thing was that after his return I still saw much less of him than I had hoped, because even in the evenings, when we might have taken a stroll together with the dogs, or I might have watched him at polo, I invariably had to be with Prince Henry so that the nurse could take time off.

A month before William's death, Richard married Birgitte van Deurs. The wedding took place at Barnwell rather than at Birgitte's home in Denmark, so that Prince Henry could be present, at least for the reception. The Queen Mother and Princess Margaret were among those who came, and William was best man. Prince Henry took part in the reception as far as he was able, looking on from his wheelchair in the drawing room. A month or so before the wedding Richard, Birgitte and I had joined William in Kenya for a brief and happy holiday. I had stayed at Deloraine while they travelled around the country.

I think William would have married quite soon himself had he lived. I do not think he had really wanted to marry before, and consequently had found it safer to have girlfriends who tended to be older than himself and already married. When he came back he was resigned to leading a more settled life, doing whatever the Queen expected of him. I am sure he would have married a suitable girl in due course. He was always such a restless, active person that I have often wondered if he had some premonition that his life was destined to be short.

I was at Barnwell the day his plane crashed. He was taking part in an air race up north. One of the other competitors flew straight over with the news as soon as it happened. He was in a terrible state, having been a staunch friend of my son. I never knew whether to tell Prince Henry or not, but I think he understood from watching the television. I was completely stunned and have never been quite the same since, though I have tried to persuade myself that it was better to have known and lost him than never to have had him at all.

At this time Princess Alice, in bed with a bad cough, happened to be with us for her annual visit to Barnwell. No one could have been of more comfort to me at such a time. When in South Africa she had received news that her son Rupert Trematon had been badly hurt in a car accident while touring with a friend in France. It would have taken two to three weeks to reach him, travelling by boat and train. He died within a few days. I realised that she knew only too well how I was feeling. I cried by her bedside and we said some prayers together. I then went for a long walk with Richard, Birgitte and the dogs. There seemed nothing better to do.

On our return I found my oldest cousin, Sir David Scott, had driven over from Boughton with a letter of sympathy, having heard the news on his television. His only son had been killed with the Army in North Africa at the age of nineteen. His letter brought to mind my many friends who had suffered likewise and been so brave and uncomplaining. Letters of condolence were overwhelming. I realised through them that sympathy is as great or even deeper than love or admiration.

William was always so bold and adventurous that even if he had not killed himself flying, it would probably have happened later in some other way. There is a commemorative plaque in the church at Barnwell and another one put up by the locals in the church of the little Staffordshire village where the accident happened. There is also an oak tree planted on the spot. They asked us not have a memorial there, because it would have caused traffic-jams at a rather dangerous corner of the road. I had had a great number of interesting letters from William, and some of these were incorporated into a book of memoirs written by his friends and edited by Giles St Aubyn, who had taught him history at Eton.

The last years of Prince Henry's life caused much distress and concern to me and my sons, and to Prince Henry's many friends and relations. There was little anyone could do except to give him every attention and comfort possible. Help in this way came from Sister Anne Greville, an Irish nurse, recommended to us by Alice Saxby. Sister Anne tended him with great devotion, and with her sense of fun could make him smile and laugh and look quite happy at times. She became almost as one of the family during those seven years, and like us was to suffer a sad loss. Her young sister was killed in a car accident in Ireland. She made friends with a New Zealander who was helping in our dairy; they married and after Prince Henry's death went to farm in Ireland. It was a great relief to me to be able to leave Prince Henry in such safe-keeping while I went off on my many public engagements.

When York House was taken over by the Lord Chamberlain's Office in 1970, the Queen had most kindly offered me the part of Kensington Palace lately occupied by Princess Marina, Duchess of Kent. The move from one home to the other was quite an undertaking and added to my already complicated life – it seemed strange having a house filled with my husband's belongings, and yet know he was unable to see it and be there with me. I tried to tell him all about it but he took no interest. I suppose he was incapable of caring by then. When William returned home from Japan in 1970 he had his own rooms and stayed there when not abroad or at Barnwell. Richard at this time had his own house in Camden near his office.

I stayed in London as short a time as possible and only when necessary for official functions. A visit to Japan during the two years that William was in Tokyo as Second Secretary with our Embassy was something I much wanted to do, but I dared not leave Prince Henry for the length of time necessary to make the journey worthwhile. Some consolation at this time was that his illness forced me to rest while sitting with him during Nurse's 'time off', and enabled me to do a great deal of embroidery which I much enjoyed. I also found some sort of peaceful happiness driving around the farm with him and all the dogs, while the surrounding scenery changed each year from brown to green and finally gold. When harvest time arrived and the great machines went back and forth we would sit and watch for ages. It seemed to please and satisfy Prince Henry and in some strange way I found it very soothing. He died two years after William, on 10 June, 1974.

Epilogue

Prince Henry no longer with me, William no longer around – no more annual holidays in Scotland, no horses to ride – I seemed bereft of so much that had brought happiness into my life. Thankfully I still had Richard, now married to Birgitte, and the welcome arrival of three grandchildren in the years to follow. Nevertheless my life in the future had obviously got to alter. I thought I might retire to Barnwell and in obscurity take again to my painting and tend to my garden and my dogs – Prince Henry's labrador, William's labrador, my three Australian terriers – and, not least, the parrot. As the days and weeks went by, however, the numbness of loss began to fade and I became conscious of the many public engagements I had previously promised to fulfil. The idea of retiring to Barnwell receded. I took up my royal responsibilities again, sustained by the continued warmth and kindness of the reception I met with everywhere.

Throughout my public life I have often wondered why such crowds should come to welcome me, both in my own country and the Commonwealth overseas. Was it to see what clothes I might be wearing? Or if I had a pretty face? Or was it that I represented something that lay deep-rooted in their hearts, a loyal and loving respect for any member of their royal family? This last I know is the true answer. To anyone who reads this book and been one of those people in crowds which have gathered to welcome me on such countless occasions, I would like to say thank you here for all the help and confidence you have given me.

The vow I made as a Girl Guide 'to serve God and the King and to do my best to help others at all times' has stood me in good stead over the sixty-seven years since I took it. I am glad to think of all the goodness that must have come about thanks to the many, many thousands of other Girl Guides and members of the Girls' Brigade, of which I am Joint Patron, who have a similar motto. I wish more recognition could be given by our Press to people who sacrifice their spare time for the benefit of others, while much that one would rather not hear about, gets written about at length. I only hope that my visits around the country may have given some encouragement to these many unselfish and patriotic people. I have so often returned home inspired by their efforts and grateful for having been able to join with their beneficiaries in giving them thanks and congratulations.

After endless tours abroad I felt no desire to travel far afield, apart from visits to one or other of my four regiments. However, persuaded by my son and daughter-in-law, I did pluck up my courage and venture on my third visit to Australia, taking my two grandchildren and their Nannie to join their parents. It was a long and tiring journey for children of four and one and an ancient Grannie, but we arrived safe and well in Sydney. Having handed over my grandchildren to their parents I then went off entirely on my own to three of the States – not even a maid or lady-in-waiting in attendance – to visit old friends. In no other country could I have done this so easily or with such a sense of freedom. It was a complete contrast with my previous existence there; I felt like a bird escaped from a cage.

I spent a weekend at Government House, Canberra, where the Governor kindly arranged a tea party of people who had been there during our stay in 1945 and 1946. It was lovely to see them again and to look at the snapshots some of them brought along to remind me of old times. A tour of the city was also arranged for me. I could hardly recognise it, so great was the change. I had known much of it as open spaces and avenues of young trees, and with a few houses here and there, half a cathedral and most of the main buildings only temporary.

Early in 1981 I ventured once more overseas – this time to Kenya in company with a cousin of Pam Scott, who like myself had happy memories of Deloraine, enjoyed water colour painting and was equally in need of sunshine and a rest. It was an admirable arrangement and Pam did everything possible to ensure a perfect holiday for both of us. This included three days at Island Camp in the middle of Lake Baringo – peaceful and beautiful with every comfort available for the twenty or so tourists it can accommodate. I also managed to visit a few remaining friends from the old days, who preferred, despite the many changes, to spend the rest of their time there rather than to live anywhere else.

As we travelled around I could not help regretting the absence of the lovely cedar trees, flame trees and podo-carpus that were in such abundance when I first came to Kenya. I was told they had been cut down to make charcoal to sell to the Arabs. I missed also the attractive thatch-roofed rondavels in which the Africans used to live, so often replaced by ugly little houses with corrugated iron roofs. I felt sure they could not be nearly so cool inside. Missing also was the wildlife that used to make one's journey so full of interest: animals of all sorts and sizes that used to peer from behind bushes, dart across the road or stampede in hordes away over the surrounding plains. Few remain now, and I imagine that those that do, will soon have to flee to the nearest Game Reserve if they are to be safe from the shotguns of hungry Africans. The birds, mercifully, did seem to have survived, and to see and hear them again was alone worth the journey. Lovely as ever also was the garden at Deloraine, a blaze of poinsettias and bougainvillaeas mingling with other exotic shrubs, some of which I had probably helped to plant fifty years before.

Later in the year there was the joyous occasion of the Royal Wedding and the wedding of my great nephew Richard Dalkeith, and in December a party for my eightieth birthday. Richard's marriage to Elizabeth Kerr gave me an excuse to visit Bowhill again. I and my family all stayed there and my elder grand-daughter Davina was a bridesmaid, looking adorable in a frilly white dress copied from an old family picture. With 'Bizza' the bride also from a Border family, the Lothians of Monteviot, the guest list included many of my old Scotch friends, as well as others from Northamptonshire and beyond.

Dalkeith Chapel was chosen for the wedding ceremony, and for the reception an enormous marquee was erected on the lawn between the chapel and the house. Today the house is occupied by a firm making computers but for this special occasion they very kindly let the family use two of the main rooms. The rooms looked somewhat different from when I had last seen them, but a few family portraits hung up for the day and a mass of flowers restored something of their former glory. There were so many old friends I had not seen for years and so much news to exchange that my voice eventually ceased to function! I thought it wiser to return home with the children and so missed the dancing which ended the party in true Scotch style.

Shortly before Christmas my son and daughter-in-law gave an eightieth birthday party for me at St James's Palace. I was amazed to discover I had so many friends still around. When the day arrived, in spite of the heavy snow, over 550 guests managed to come. For many, I know, it had required quite an effort. Leaving an empty house with no one to look after the dogs, not to mention the expense and difficulties of travel, can be a problem for the elderly today. I was greatly touched so many made the effort personally to wish me a 'Happy Birthday'.

When I talked to my nieces and their friends about the days of my youth they seemed always intrigued and amused. Indeed they implored me to put the stories down on paper so that they should not be lost. 'Better still,' they said, 'write a book.' So I started to do so – not intending to cover more than the years before my marriage. It seemed to me Dr Noble Frankland, in his official biography of my husband, *Prince Henry, Duke of Gloucester*, had written as much as anyone would want to know about the rest. However, my editor persuaded me to carry on, saying that people would be interested and like to hear more of me! I only hope he is right.

The lives of my grandchildren will be so very different, and when they grow up it may prove hard for them to believe that all I have written is true. It seems incredible, for instance, that Barnwell as recently as 1950 accommodated a butler, valet, footman, pantry boy, odd-man, ladies' maid, cook, two kitchen maids, head housemaid and two under housemaids to do the same amount of work as is now accomplished by my maid, my butler, (an ex-garden boy) with one young assistant, a cook straight from college and two 'dailies'. And so it is with many of my friends and acquaintances, amongst them my nephew Johnnie Buccleuch, whose family homes are now all open to the public, with the vast kitchens as much an object of interest to the many visitors as the pictures and furniture. He and his family live mostly in small, easy-to-heat rooms in a corner of their homes. They have not only made it possible for others to see and appreciate the contents of these great houses but have made many changes outside, adding adventure playgrounds for the amusement of the young and picnic spots for the benefit of tourists and visitors to the countryside.

Now in my eighty-first year and failing in sight and limbs I know I too must resign myself to a more restful existence. I must retire, with regrets but also with relief, from the many commitments of the past years. I know that I am most fortunate to have Barnwell for my retirement. The old place is getting somewhat shabby and worn and the once lovely garden is a mass of overgrown shrubs. Flowers, once so carefully tended, now have to struggle to compete with the nettles and other weeds. But all around are reminders of past happiness and friends, living and dead, to which I can turn in my mind as a relief from the endless horrors of the world. To me it is an abode of quiet peace and contentment and trust. I pray that it may remain so for my family in the years to come.

Acknowledgements

I am more than grateful to my sisters Sybil and Mary and our old butler, Mr Rowland, now over ninety years of age, whose early memories added to mine have been of great help in writing this book.

And to John Sebastian McEwen for his patience and help in editing this manuscript.

Index